MW00413695

Nourishment
from the Word

Select Studies in
Reformed Doctrine

Praise for 𝔑ourishment *from the* 𝔚ORD . . .

Nourishment from the Word: Select Studies in Reformed Doctrine, is a welcomed collection of shorter writings by the noted Reformed theologian, Dr. Kenneth L. Gentry. Dr. Gentry puts forth concise theological arguments and well-articulated distinctions of Reformed theological thought on a variety of subjects. Every student of the Holy Scriptures will greatly benefit from reading this book.

—Dr. Kenneth Gary Talbot
President
Whitefield College and Theological Seminary, Lakeland, Florida

I have found the material in this volume to be of tremendous help to my own theological study. Whenever I forget about the Scriptural details of these issues, I find myself pulling these chapters back out, because Dr. Gentry is so organized, concise, and to the point about what really matters.

—Brian Godawa
Author, *Hollywood Worldviews:*
Watching Films with Wisdom and Discernment, Los Angeles, California

From the dawning of a six-day creation to the world's ending, Dr. Gentry's brilliant insights are always well worth pondering. This small collection of writings contains some of his most profound, God-honoring thinking. Masterful understanding of scripture combined with sound logic causes one to deeply ponder his conclusions. Thorough and incisive in his research and argumentation, Dr. Gentry epitomizes the Spirit-inspired man who has dedicated himself to loving the LORD with his entire mind.

—John David McPeak
Lieutenant Colonel, Ret. U.S. Army
M.S., Strategic Intelligence, Joint Military Intelligence College,
Bolling Air Force Base, Washington, DC

It is impossible to love God with our minds if they are empty. This volume, with clarity, relevance, and wit, equips Christians to develop minds so that they cease being empty-headed children, and instead can in their "thinking be mature" (1 *Cor.* 14:20). Even where I disagree with my learned friend, the cogency of his analysis remains compelling.

—Jeffery J. Ventrella, J.D.
Senior Vice-President,
Strategic Training, Alliance Defense Fund, Mesa, Arizona

Dr. Gentry has constructed a wonderful resource on key ecclesiastical and doctrinal issues. The format is easy to read, the organization is clear and succinct, and the argumentation compelling. This book will be a helpful tool to pastors and laypersons alike.

—Rev. Dan Dodds
Minister of Counseling and Care
Woodruff Road Presbyterian Church (PCA), Greenville, South Carolina

Nourishment
from the WORD

SELECT STUDIES *in*
REFORMED DOCTRINE

Kenneth L. Gentry, Jr.

Ventura, California
2008

Nourishment from the Word:
Select Studies in Reformed Doctrine
by Kenneth L. Gentry, Jr.

Copyright © 2008 by Gentry Family Trust UDT April 2, 1999

Kenneth Gentry Ministries • www.KennethGentry.com
Previously published as eight separate booklets:
Biblical Issues Series

International Standard Book Number: 978-0-9796736-4-1

Library of Congress Control Number: 2008929712

Theology Editor: Ron Kirk

Proofing: Kimberley Winters

Typography and Design: Desta Garrett, www.dg-ink.net

Except where otherwise noted,
Scripture quotations are taken from the New American Standard Bible®,
Copyright © 1960, 1962, 1963, 1968, 1971, 1972, 1973, 1975, 1977, 1995
by The Lockman Foundation. Used by permission.

Scripture quotations marked "NKJV™" are taken from the New King James Version®.
Copyright © 1982 by Thomas Nelson, Inc. Used by permission. All rights reserved.

No part of this publication may be reproduced, stored in a retrieval system,
or transmitted, in any form or by any means—electronic, mechanical,
photocopy, recording, or otherwise—without prior written permission.

Printed in the United States of America.

Published by

NORDSKOG PUBLISHING, INC.
2716 Sailor Avenue
Ventura, California 93001, USA
1-805-642-2070 • 1-805-276-5129

www.NordskogPublishing.com

Christian Small Publishers Association

To Dr. Lee Hahnlen

A good theologian, gracious pastor,

and dear friend

About the Author

ENNETH L. GENTRY, JR., B.A., M.DIV., TH.M., TH.D., is a Reformed theologian and a member of the Presbyterian Church in America. He was born May 3, 1950, in Chattanooga, Tennessee. He and his wife Melissa were married in July of 1971, and have three grown children, all who have confessed Jesus Christ as Lord and God.

Ken received his B.A. in Biblical Studies from Tennessee Temple University (1973, cum laude). After graduating, he enrolled at Grace Theological Seminary in Winona Lake, Indiana. After two years at Grace Seminary (1973-1975), he left dispensationalism, having become convinced of a covenant and Reformed theology. He transferred to Reformed Theological Seminary in Jackson, Mississippi (1975-1977). Upon completing studies at Reformed Theological Seminary, he was awarded the M.DIV. in 1977. After several years of pastoral ministry, he earned a TH.M. (1986) and a TH.D. (1987, magna cum laude) from Whitefield Theological Seminary, both in the field of New Testament.

While at Reformed Theological Seminary, he studied under Greg L. Bahnsen, a leading presuppositional apologist. Though Gentry initially resisted the distinctive ethical and eschatological views of Bahnsen, he was eventually persuaded of both theonomic ethics and postmillennial eschatology and became a staunch co-defender of them with Bahnsen. Over the years, he developed a close friendship with Bahnsen, often lecturing with him in conferences and co-writing a book with him (*House Divided: The Break-up of Dispensational Theology*). He eventually joined the staff of Bahnsen's Southern California Center for Christian Studies, and contributed to the *festschrift* in honor of Bahnsen, titled: *The Standard Bearer*.

Ken has authored or co-authored some twenty-plus books and is perhaps best known for his book *Before Jerusalem Fell*, which argues that the Book of Revelation was written before the destruction of Jerusalem in A.D. 70. He holds that many of the dramatic events in Revelation correspond to the persecution of Christians under the Roman imperium as well as to the Jewish War against Rome which resulted in the destruction of the Jewish temple.

Gentry is the Executive Director of GoodBirth Ministries, a non-profit religious educational ministry, "committed to sponsoring, subsidizing, and advancing serious Christian scholarship and education." He is also the Director of NiceneCouncil.com, a Christian apologetics Web site.

From the Publisher

This book is created for all serious Christians desiring to dig deeper into the Bible and find the truth, as the Truth will set us free. We need to be consuming the meat and not just the milk of theology. Wisdom is the principle thing, so says the Word of God; it comes from the fear of the Lord, from knowledge (Epistemology), understanding of reality (Ontology), and God's Law (Theonomy), developing our faith by the hearing and reading of God's revelation. Together we dig for God's nuggets of gold.

Dr. Kenneth Gentry, an astute, brilliant Bible Scholar and devoted man of God, helps the reader find those golden nuggets—dissecting, comparing Scripture with Scripture, deciphering the context and time of events—all in a systematic theological manner empowered by the Holy Spirit. His background in the Reformed tradition of the faith (see "About the Author"), his intentional deep study of Holy Writ, and his precise and gentle, loving style of communicating, makes this book a must for students who want to follow Jesus lovingly, obediently, and wisely.

Here is a tiny sampling of the tasty morsels you will discover in this book from Dr. Gentry's informed pen:

"A growing understanding of the Bible comes only through reading it, systematizing it, studying it, hearing it expounded, and applying it." (Chapter One, page 8)

"The fact that the truth of Scripture is of no 'private interpretation' is a foundational principle of creedal theology. No interpreter of Scripture works alone; we all must build on the past labors of godly predecessors." (Chapter One, page 10)

"Reformed Christians are a 'people of The Book.' We firmly believe that both the Old and New Testaments are God-breathed and profitable for God's people. Though we may easily discern obvious progress and development in Scripture, the Bible is, nevertheless, *one* Book." (Chapter Two, page 16)

"Actually the defense of Christianity is simple: we argue the impossibility of the contrary. Those who assault the Christian system must actually assume the Christian system to do so. In fact, atheism assumes theism." (Chapter Five, page 90)

"But I believe [this] sufficiently demonstrates the validity of the Westminster Confession, which declares: 'It pleased God the Father, Son, and Holy Ghost, for the manifestation of the glory of His eternal power, wisdom, and goodness, in the beginning, to create, or make of nothing, the world, and all things therein whether visible or invisible, in the space of six days; and all very good.'" (Chapter Six, page 99)

"Thus, the theme of Revelation is the execution of God's divorce decree against Israel, her subsequent capital punishment and cremation, followed by His turning to take a new bride, the Church." (Chapter Eight, page 153)

My personal gratitude to Dr. Ken Gentry for allowing us to republish his work in one volume, dispensing sound exegetical expository of

Holy Scripture, helping all of us to learn, grow, and enjoy this "Nourishment from the Word" in these "Select Studies in Reformed Doctrine" all to the glory of God. As Dr. Gentry affirms in his initial chapter: "It is fundamentally necessary to hold as one's credo: 'I believe Jesus is Lord.'"

—Gerald Christian Nordskog
Publisher

Contents

₽REFACE

e live in an age of doctrinal confusion and spiritual anemia. The Christian airwaves are dominated by charismatics, Christian bookstores are purveyors of froth and trinkets, and Christian churches are more interested in numbers than in truth. This doctrinal declension is even affecting Reformed churches, once known for doctrinal fidelity. Gary North commented that the reason Presbyterian churches no longer preach doctrine is because the Baptist church across the street has a bigger gymnasium. Sadly, God's people are "destroyed for lack of knowledge" (Hos. 4:6).

This book presents in collected form eight studies published separately as the *Biblical Issues Series*. In these studies, I touch on eight themes that are significant for the Reformed Christian's understanding of his doctrinal heritage which is strongly rooted in Biblical truth. I have organized these in two sections: the first dealing with "Church Issues" and the second on "Doctrinal Issues."

The first section on Church Issues relates to important matters framing some distinctives of the Reformed church itself. Chapter One studies the issue of "Creeds and Confessions." Reformed Christianity recognizes the organic nature of the church, which leads to our organic understanding of and commitment to the truth. That is, we recognize that we are not a law unto ourselves, we are not islands in the stream. Rather we are a part of the flowing stream of historic Christianity itself. Hence, we give credence to creeds, you might say. Reformed Christians need to understand the Biblical warrant for and the theological value of creeds and confessions.

Chapter Two explains and defends a distinctively Reformed understanding of "Infant Baptism." Our children are the seed of the covenant and members of the church of Jesus Christ. They are not outsiders who are visiting the church until some time when they reach an "age of accountability." Reformed Christians must recognize this truth as vitally important, not only for understanding the Biblical nature of church membership, but the covenantal significance of children in the Christian life.

Chapter Three focuses on "Baptismal Mode." Since our doctrine is covenantal, our method of baptism is rooted in Old Testament imagery, which repeatedly emphasizes ceremonial sprinklings and pourings. Whereas many an evangelical church claims to be a "New Testament church," a Reformed church should claim to be a "whole Bible church." Furthermore, in that water baptism pictures Spirit baptism, I show that the Bible presents both baptisms as coming down from above and by means of pouring. Reformed Christians need to understand the Biblical warrant for why we baptize as we do.

Chapter Four reckons with the matter of "Tongues-Speaking," which is a widely popular, broadcast-dominating phenomenon afflicting many churches today. This chapter looks into the various Biblical passages touching on tongues-speaking. In it I show that the very form of modern tongues-speaking [glossalia] differs from Biblical tongues. The reason for this confusion is largely related to the fact that the miraculous nature of Biblical tongues confines them to the apostolic church and the first century. Reformed Christians need to understand that their lack of tongues-speaking is not an indicator of a lack of spirituality and that the popularity of tongues today is another sign of confusion in the church.

The second section of this book contains four studies on "Doctrinal Issues" that are significant for the modern Reformed church's self-understanding. Chapter Five considers the proper method of "Defending the Faith." The Reformed faith does not argue that Christianity is the best option among competing worldviews. Rather it insists that it is the only rational option because of the two-leveled nature of reality: the Creator and the creature. It does not argue that Christianity is possibly or even probably true, but that it is absolutely and certainly true. Reformed Christians need to defend the Biblical faith in a way that flows from the very nature of that faith itself.

Chapter Six presents the argument for "Six Day Creation." Six-day creation is a major contemporary controversy pitting the Christian worldview against secularism. Not only that, it even differs from some popular compromises promoted within Reformed circles themselves. The very integrity of the Bible and the foundation of the Christian worldview are at stake in this debate. Reformed Christians must understand the clear and compelling Biblical argument for the method of creation which has been revealed to us by the Creator Himself.

Chapter Seven considers the proper Reformed understanding of the role of God's Law in the new covenant era. This chapter demonstrates that the primary confession of Presbyterianism, the Westminster Confession of Faith, affirms the continuing validity of God's Law today. Given our cultural relativism and its antipathy to absolute standards for ethics, this is an important matter for promoting the Christian worldview. Reformed Christians must understand their historic commitment to God's Law as the absolute, God-revealed standard for ethics.

Chapter Eight highlights the most debated book in Scripture, "The Revelation of Jesus Christ." Unfortunately, no Reformed consensus exists on the book of Revelation (it has even been lamented that wherever you find five commentaries on Revelation you will discover six views of Revelation). Yet the modern evangelical mind is saturated with what the Reformed community does almost universally denounce: premillennialism. In this chapter, I show that Revelation actually deals with the beginning of Christian history, not its end. The contemporary church has literally turned the Revelation of Jesus Christ upside down. Reformed Christians must apprehend the true meaning of Revelation in order to help fellow evangelicals see the error of their premillennial analysis.

Each of these chapters contains material quite important for bracing against the tides of confusion lapping at Christian foundations. I hope that this book will serve not only for your own private study, but for group Bible studies in your particular church or local community. Paul writes to Timothy in a way that we would do well to emulate: "In pointing out these things to the brethren, you will be a good servant of Christ Jesus, constantly nourished on the words of the faith and of the sound doctrine which you have been following" (1 Tim. 4:6).

These studies were originally published in separate booklets comprising the *Biblical Issues Series.* I would like to thank Jerry Nordskog and Nordskog Publishing, Inc. for combining these studies in one volume. As noted above, Paul urges us to be "constantly nourished on the words of the faith." Truly Nordskog's commitment to publishing "meaty, tasty, and easily digestible books" on Christian theology maintains that Pauline concern for nourishment. Nordskog is a welcome endeavor in a publishing market largely confused and confusing.

—Kenneth L. Gentry, Jr., Th.M., Th.D.

Executive Director, GoodBirth Ministries
www.GoodBirthMinistries.com

Director, NiceneCouncil.Com
www.NiceneCouncil.com

Church

Issues

CHAPTER ONE

Creeds and Confessions

A Defense of the Usefulness of Creeds

We live in a non-creedal age. By and large, conservative Christians diminish the importance of creeds and confessions of faith. As a matter of fact, many noncreedalists do not simply dismiss creeds as unimportant for maintaining Biblical Christianity, they decry them as positively antithetical to it. Such a position is not simply "non-creedal," but rather "anti-creedal."

Many factors are at work generating this anti-creedal sentiment today. Among these we may list the following: an increasing permeation of society with a relativistic, existential concern for the moment; a loss of a sense of the significance of history; a democratic concern for non-coercion and individual freedom of belief; a pervasive tendency to simplification—as well as other considerations. But at the forefront of the widespread fundamentalist disapprobation of creeds is the fear that the framing of creeds undermines the sufficiency of Scripture. The cry "no creed but the Bible" appears to re-assert the primacy of the Bible in religious affairs in such a way as to totally discredit creedalism.

In one book leveling a critical assault on creedalism, we find the following statement: "To arrive at truth we must dismiss religious prejudices from heart to mind. We must let God speak for Himself. . . . To let God be true means to let God have the say as to what is the truth that sets men free. It means to accept His word, the Bible, as the truth. Our appeal is to the Bible for truth." The same book spurns creeds as "man-made traditions," "the precepts of men," and "opinions."

These sentiments well represent many anti-creedalists, especially those within fundamentalist circles. The fundamentalist view of creeds is important for two reasons. Fundamentalism is not only one of the dominant forces in American Christianity today, but is also the spiritual blood-sister of Reformed Christianity. Consequently, conservative Reformed Christians ought to have a proper understanding of the status and role of creeds in order to defend the Biblical integrity of their faith.

This brief study will introduce two particular aspects of creedalism: (1) The relation of creed to Scripture, and (2) The function of creeds in Christianity.

The Relation of Creed to Scripture

At the very outset of the discussion, it is imperative to recognize that creedal standards are not independent assertions of truth. Nor are they truth claims on a par with Scripture. Creeds are derived from and subordinate to the Bible. The Bible is the only source and standard of Christian truth since it is the infallible, inerrant Word of the Living God.

Understanding the original meaning of the word "creed" may be helpful for dispelling some anti-creedal concerns. The English word *creed* is derived from the Latin *credo*, which simply means: "I believe." A creed, then, is a statement of faith. As such, a creed no more diminishes the authority of God's Word than do statements such as "I believe in God" or "I believe in the resurrection of Christ." As a matter of fact, such statements *are* creeds—albeit, brief, informal ones. Anyone who thinks of God in a particular way has "encreeded" a view of God, whether or not he reduces this "creed" to writing. Surely this in no way diminishes the primacy or the centrality of the Bible.

Furthermore, some argue that a creed reduces the authority of the Bible by implying its inadequacy. They ask why we need a creed if we have the Bible. If such a concern were valid, we could argue with equal force that a minister's sermonic exposition of Christ's words implies that Christ's words are inadequate as they stand. Such is patently false.

Those who fault Presbyterian subscription to the Westminster Standards (or the subscription of Congregationalists and Baptists to closely related Standards) should be made to realize that the Westminster Confession is self-consciously derived from and subordinate to the Bible. It not only amply demonstrates and vigorously maintains its utter dependence upon Scripture in its opening chapter, but it allows—in fact, *encourages*—appeal from itself to its authority, the Bible.

Witness paragraphs four and ten from its initial chapter:

• "The authority of the Holy Scripture, for which it ought to be believed, and obeyed, dependeth not upon the testimony of any man, or Church, but wholly upon God (who is truth itself) the author thereof: and therefore it is to be received, because it is the Word of God." (WCF 1:4)

• "The supreme judge, by which all controversies of religion are to be determined, and all decrees of councils, opinions of ancient writers, doctrines of men, and private spirits, are to be examined, and in whose sentence we are to rest, can be no other but the Holy Spirit speaking in the Scripture." (WCF 1:10)

Furthermore, at WCF 31:3 the Confession speaks of the subordinate authority of all ecclesiastical creeds. Such creedal formulations are to be heeded only "if consonant with the Word of God." Thus, the Westminster Confession of Faith, as a proper creed, actually vouchsafes the supreme, unparalleled authority of Scripture.

Certainly no law in Scripture explicitly commands "Thou shalt frame creeds." Nevertheless, the impetus and mandate for creeds derive from good and necessary inferences deduced from Scripture. We can demonstrate this in a variety of ways, three of which will suffice for our present purpose.

First, the Biblical call for a public affirmation of faith serves as the prime impetus to creedalism. The essence of Christian duty is to be a witness (Acts 1:8). This requires publicly defining the exact identity of that to which the Christian is witness. Obviously reciting the entire Scripture record at a given opportunity of witness is not possible. Furthermore, only God can look into the hearts of individuals to ascertain their innermost faith (1 Sam. 16:7; Luke 16:15). Thus, for others to know of an individual's personal faith it is necessary to put it into words. "With the heart man believes, resulting in righteousness, and with the mouth he confesses, resulting in salvation" (Rom. 10:10). Hence, we see the necessity of a creed in *defining the content of belief.*

Second, mini-creeds are preserved in the Biblical record of apostolic Christianity itself. The very seeds of a full-blown creedalism are sown in the apostolic era via terse statements of faith which are widely employed. Perhaps the most familiar of these rudimentary creeds is the recurring one embedded in such texts as Acts 10:36; Romans 10:9; 1 Corinthians 12:3; and Philippians 2:11: "Jesus is Lord." This eminently important statement embodies—"encreeds," if you will—a particular way of viewing Jesus Christ. It is fundamentally necessary to hold as one's *credo:* "I believe Jesus is Lord."

Third, within the Biblical record we find early ecclesiastical assemblies re-casting already known truths to ensure their accurate preservation and transmission. Acts 15 is the *locus classicus* in this regard. There the Church restates "justification by faith" in response to a Christian-Pharisaic pressure demanding the circumcision of Gentile converts (cf. Acts 15:1).

After noting several such situations in Scripture, nineteenth-century Scottish Presbyterian theologian James Bannerman observes:

> Such, within the age of inspiration itself, are the remarkable examples we have of the necessity, growing out of the circumstances of the Church and its members, that arose at different times for recasting the doctrines of Scripture in a new mold, and exhibiting or explaining it afresh under forms of language and expression more precisely fitted to meet and counteract the error of the times.[1]

Thus the concept of creedalism is a Scriptural one that in no way diminishes the authority of Scripture or implies its inadequacy.

The Function of Creeds in Christianity

The above study intimates a variety of creedal functions. The following enumeration and explication of six important functions of creeds will focus on their specifically ecclesiastical functions. Broader socio-cultural implications flow forth from creedalism, but these are beyond

the purview of the present study (see R. J. Rushdoony, *Th*
of Social Order).

First, *creeds serve as a basis for ecclesiastical fellowship and*
Whenever two walk together they must be agreed (Amos 3:3) for a "house
divided against itself cannot stand" (Matt. 12:25). Community labors are
better performed and "body life" is more consistently maintained within
that church which possesses a homogeneity of faith (Eph. 4:5, 11-13). And
it is imperative that the particular content of that fundamental faith be
known, as in a written creed.

Non-creedal fundamentalism is both internally inconsistent at the
theoretical level and seriously endangered at the practical level. Its theoretical inconsistency is manifest in the internal contradiction of the very
statement "no creed but the Bible." *This statement itself is a creed.* It says,
in effect: "I believe (*credo*) in no creed." That is, "My creed is that there
be no creed." Furthermore, this theoretical position is not amenable to
practice. Even the notoriously anti-creedal Church of Christ sect requires
some sort of implied statement of belief from persons seeking positions of
authority in its fellowship. A paedo-baptist or a Five Point Calvinist will
simply never be allowed in its ministry.

Ironically, non-creedalism possesses inherent dangers in that in principle such a position allows almost any doctrine into a church. The
anti-creedal quotations in the third paragraph of this study are pious
sounding and widely representative of many churches. Unfortunately,
the statements are drawn from *Let God Be True*, a publication of the
Jehovah's Witnesses. The essence of the citation could well be reduced
to: "No creed but the Bible." Yet despite the Jehovah's Witnesses's adoption of the same principle (no creed) and the same authority (the Bible),
they are unacceptable to orthodox churches. Obviously there is more
to orthodoxy than the claim "no creed but the Bible." And once you
go beyond "no creed but the Bible" to probe one's faith you are thereby
establishing a creed, a statement of faith.

Southern Presbyterian theologian Robert L. Dabney aptly comments:
"As man's mind is notoriously fallible, and professed Christians who claim
to hold the Scriptures, as they understand them, differ from each other
notoriously, some platform for union and cooperation must be adopted,

by which those who believe they are truly agreed may stand and work together."[2] Churches absolutely must provide a formal, public affirmation of their faith so their members and prospective members may know exactly where they stand. This is the function of a creed.

Second, creeds serve as tools of Christian education. Obviously the sheer volume of the Bible (1,189 chapters containing over 773,000 words) forbids its full comprehension in a moment and by every Christian—or even by one supremely gifted believer in an entire lifetime. Nevertheless, God commands His people in the Old Testament *Shema* (Deut. 6:4-25) and in the New Testament Great Commission (Matt. 28:19-20) to teach the Bible's truth to others. This teaching process necessarily deals with fundamental, selected truths at first—truths such as outlined and organized in a creed.

A growing understanding of the Bible comes only through reading it, systematizing it, studying it, hearing it expounded, and applying it. Nineteenth century Presbyterian theologian A. A. Hodge notes in his defense of creeds: "While...the Scriptures are from God, the understanding of them belongs to the part of men. Men must interpret to the best of their ability each particular part of the Scripture separately, and then combine all that the Scripture teaches upon different subjects in mutual consistency as parts of a harmonious system."[3] In short, creeds are simply expository distillations of Scripture. They summarily state the most basic themes of Scripture in order to facilitate education in them.

If a brief expository summation of the teachings of the Bible is acceptable to evangelical Christians, then creeds are legitimatized in that they fulfill that precise function. In this respect, creeds differ from doctrinal sermons only in being more exact and being more carefully compiled by several minds. Once a church encourages public teaching of the Word or publishes literature explaining it, that church has in fact made a creedal statement.

Third, creeds provide an objective, concrete standard of church discipline. As noted previously, any church having officers or teachers must require their accepting the standard of belief of that church. The position "no creed but the Bible" cannot and does not serve as a standard in any church. The fact that cultists are debarred from service in orthodox churches illustrates a creed of sorts exists.

If a church has any interpretation at all of any part of the Bible that must be held by its officers, then *ipso facto* it has a creed—even if it is unwritten. But an unwritten creed serving as a standard of discipline in such circumstances is both dishonest and dangerous. Surely it is far more open and honest to have a stable, clearly worded, publicly recognizable, formally adopted standard of belief. Then appeal can be made to this standard in situations where men are either debarred from entering the ministry or from joining a church, or are forcibly relinquished of their duties or membership on a charge of heresy.

A news article appearing in the November 21, 1980, issue of *Christianity Today* documents in a slightly different setting the danger of the disavowal of creedal discipline. The article reports that a particular church-related college had been embroiled in a controversy over a certain teacher's instruction in a human sexuality course. The reporter perceptively notes in passing: "Faculty are not required to sign a doctrinal statement, mostly because of long-standing opposition to creeds." The absence of subscription to a creed was a factor complicating the adjudication of that controversy. The voluntary subscription to a creedal standard is an effective tool of church discipline which enhances doctrinal purity by reducing equivocation on fundamental issues.

Fourth, creeds help to preserve the orthodox Christian faith in the ongoing Church. Jude 3 exhorts Christians: "Beloved, while I was making every effort to write you about our common salvation, I felt the necessity to write to you appealing that you earnestly contend for the faith which was once for all delivered to the saints."

The system of faith incorporated in the Scriptures, embodied in the Lord Jesus Christ and revealed in finality by the apostles, is "once for all delivered." It is unchanging and unchangeable. That immutable faith must be preserved from generation to generation. Creeds that are true to Scripture admirably serve to tie generations of believers together by laying down a specific set of fundamental truths.

The Scriptures carefully instruct the Church to preserve the faith. Hebrews 13:9 warns: "Do not be carried away by varied and strange teachings." Paul instructs two early church leaders in this vein. To Timothy he writes: "Retain the standard of sound words which you have heard from me, in the faith and love which are in Christ Jesus" (2 Tim. 1:13). He urges Titus carefully to see that an overseer hold "fast the faithful word which is in accord with the teaching, that he may be able to exhort in sound doctrine and to refute those who contradict" (Tit. 1:9).

Although the special, direct revelation of God ceased and the corpus of Scripture was finalized in the first century, it still remains necessary for the continuing Church to interpret and apply the completed revelation. The interpretation and application of Scripture involve a process, not an act. It has required the involvement of many devout men working through many centuries to systematize, compile, and disseminate the fundamental truths of Scripture.

The fact that the truth of Scripture is of no "private interpretation" is a foundational principle of creedal theology. No interpreter of Scripture works alone; we all must build on the past labors of godly predecessors. The interpreter or group of exegetes who agree with the historic, orthodox interpretations of the past and who find themselves in the mainstream of Christian thought are not suspect. Rather, the one who presents novel deviations from historic Christendom deserves careful scrutiny. Creeds help to preserve the essential core of true Christian faith from generation to generation.

The Apostle Paul expresses his fear that some within the Corinthian church are in danger of being "led astray from the simplicity and purity of devotion to Christ" by subtle craftiness (2 Cor. 11:3). The same concern must provoke the Church today to guard the central elements of Christian truth from distortion. In terms of a creed's function in this regard, A. A. Hodge remarks that the real question is not, as often pretended, "between the word of God and the creed of man, but between the tried and proved faith of the collective body of God's people, and the private judgment and the unassisted wisdom of the individual objector."[4]

Fifth, creeds offer a witness to the truth to those outside the Church. In many ways the Church is to be the "light of the world" (Matt. 5:14). Various methods are available for carrying the light of the truth into the world. The framing of a well-composed creed is one significant means.

Basically the question which outsiders ask the Church is: "What do you believe?" Non-creedal churches reply: "We believe the Bible." Creedal churches respond further: "We believe the Bible, and we have written out exactly what it is that we believe the Bible teaches, which is...." The primary question, "What do you believe?" (to which the proper response is "the Bible") must be followed up by the more searching question: "What do you believe the Bible teaches?"

Creeds witness to the truth to those outside the bounds of the covenant community by: (1) clearly outlining and explicating the fundamental assertions of Christianity; (2) seriously warning against misbelief; (3) vigorously defending the truth from corruptions; (4) boldly witnessing to the unity and order of the Christian system; (5) carefully demonstrating the continuity and immutability of the historic Christian faith; (6) publicly demonstrating the rational, objective content of Christian truth (as against misperceptions such as a belief that Christian faith is a mystic, blind leap); and so on.

Sixth, creeds provide a standard by which to judge new teachings arising within the Church. This function obviously relates to ideas embodied in several of the above-mentioned functions. But its usefulness in an age prone to cultism deserves separate and especial emphasis. "Christian" cults are a particularly dangerous phenomenon in that they proselytize by appeal to Scripture. Cults have been called "the unpaid bills of the Church." Creeds guard against cultic aberrations by clearly providing a proper interpretation of essential truths. The more clearly, systematically, and concisely truth is stated, the less likely people are to stray from it in the fog of deception.

Maintaining a standard of truth in the Church is in keeping with apostolic example. 1 John 4:1a warns: "Beloved, do not believe every spirit, but test the spirits to see whether they are from God." In the following two verses, John provides a specific test point or standard of judgment (creed): "Every spirit that confesses that Jesus Christ has come in the flesh is from God; and every spirit that does not confess Jesus is not from God" (1 John 4:2a-3a). This credo was formulated in response to a particular error infecting the early Church: *docetism* taught that Christ was really not a material person, but only *seemed* (Gk.: *dokeo*) to have a material body. We could cite numerous references following the pattern of 1 John 4 (e.g., Gal. 1:8, 9; 2 John 10; Rev. 2:2; etc.).

Because of the relentless assaults on the Church from without and the internal buffetings from within, creeds are crucial defensive instruments. As Bannerman aptly observes: "Had the adoption of confessions and creeds not been a duty laid upon the Church by a regard to her own members, it would have been a necessity laid upon the Church by a regard to those not her members, but her enemies."[5]

Conclusion

We can produce a strong Biblical case in defense of creedalism. Creeds are invaluable instruments of Christian education and discipline. They in no way diminish the authority of Scripture. The decline in creedalism today in conservative Christian circles is lamentable. Anti-creedalism represents not only a literary and historical loss to society and culture, but a spiritual tragedy and doctrinal danger to the Church.

Reformed Christians need to be trained in creedal theology to bolster the historic Christian faith against the assaults of relativistic, existential, liberal, and cultic theologies current at this time. Reformed churches could curb the decline of creedalism within their own ranks and within American Christianity in general by several simple actions:

1) Local churches should distribute the Westminster Standards or some other historic confession or doctrinal creed of your church or denomination to all of your congregational families and urge its study.

2) The Christian Education program of local congregations should include the catechizing of children and youth as an ongoing function of the church.

3) New-member classes should be offered to those seeking membership within Reformed churches. These classes should at least briefly introduce and review the Westminster Standards or similar creed.

4) Ministers and Sunday-school teachers should be encouraged to expound the Standards in a systematic way and to illustrate their lessons by reference to the Confessional documents.

May the Lord bless us to know what we believe so that we might declare it to others. May we as orthodox, Bible-believing Christians regain an appreciation for the Biblical and historic utility of creeds.

Endnotes

1 James Bannerman, *The Church of Christ*. Edinburgh: Banner of Truth, rep. 1974 [1869], 1:294.

2 Robert L. Dabney, *Discussions: Evangelical and Theological*. London: Banner of Truth, 1967, 1:315.

3 A. A. Hodge, *Commentary on the Confession of Faith*. Philadelphia: Presbyterian Board of Publication and Sabbath-School Work, 1923, 19.

4 Hodge, *A Commentary of the Confession of Faith*, 21.

5 Bannerman, *The Church of Christ*, 1:301. For a thorough response to common objections against creeds, see my chapter in Keith Mathison, ed., *When Shall These Things Be?* Phillipsburg, N. J.: P and R, 2003.

CHAPTER TWO

Infant Baptism

The Biblical Rationale
for Baptizing Infants

As Christians we *must* be concerned to do all those things God commands us and to avoid those things God forbids. This should be true in every endeavor of life (1 Cor. 10:31; Matt. 4:4) since we live in the earth, which is the Lord's (Ps. 24:1; 1 Cor. 10:26, 28). Thus, it should be all the more true in the formal worship of the Lord God in His Church, for God is not pleased with innovation in worship (Lev. 10:1-3; Mark 7:8-9). We must justify Church practices from the Bible, which is the Word of the Living God (John 17:17) and the only rule God has given for faith and practice (2 Tim. 3:16-17).

Many non-Reformed Christians charge that it is improper to baptize infants. Some see infant baptism as a vestige of Roman Catholicism, expressing an undue concern for historic tradition rather than Biblical fidelity. A. H. Strong called it a "rag of Romanism" (*Systematic Theology*, 954). Alexander Campbell deemed it as among "the relics of Popery" (*Christian Baptism*, 15). John R. Rice wrote that "all modern denominations which use these customs got them from Roman Catholics" (*Bible Baptism*, 51). Others, not so much opposed to the practice, suppose that it is a mere dedicatory rite for the benefit of the parents and grandparents. This deems it no true baptism at all. Such positions are greatly misinformed.

Contrary to such views, evangelical Presbyterianism deems infant baptism a Christian duty firmly rooted in Scriptural precept and principle. Consequently, neglecting it is a serious failure of Christian duty before the Lord. Outlined below is a brief, non-technical, introductory demonstration of the Scriptural mandate obligating believers to have their infants baptized.

The Essential Unity of the Bible

Reformed Christians are a "people of The Book." We firmly believe that both the Old and New Testaments are God-breathed and profitable for God's people. Though we may easily discern obvious progress and development in Scripture, the Bible is, nevertheless, *one* Book.

The unity of Scripture can be demonstrated from a variety of angles. Let us simply note three of these.

First, the Scriptures have a unity of *purpose* overarching both testaments. As the Word of God, the Bible seeks to glorify the name of the Lord (Deut. 5:24; Ps. 8:1; Rev. 4:11; Rom. 16:27) and to show the way of salvation to men (Isa. 12:1-6; 55:1-7; Eph. 1:1-14; Rom. 1:16). These twin themes (doxology and soteriology) are constant in both parts of the Bible.

Second, the Scriptures witness to a unity of *principle* undergirding both testaments. The Law of God is God's righteous pattern for man's conduct (Exod. 20:1-17; Ps. 119; Matt. 5:17-19; Rom. 3:31; 7:12; 8:3-4,7; 1 John 3:22). The revealed Law of God is the foundational principle and source of Biblical ethics in both testaments.

Third, the Scriptures display a unity of *people* in both testaments. The New Testament people of God are a continuation and expansion of the Old Testament people. Since this concept has been so misunderstood since the mid-1800s it might be helpful to give a little fuller rehearsal of its evidence:

1) Both peoples are called a "church," or "congregation," or "assembly." These words in the original languages of Scripture are synonyms meaning "a called out gathering" (Exod. 12:6; Lev. 4:13; Jer. 26:17; Matt. 18:17; Eph. 5:23-33). The New Testament itself calls the Old Testament people a "church" (Acts 7:38; Heb. 2:12) and our "fathers" (1 Cor. 10:1).

2) The Old Testament people were set apart for the true gospel, just as are the New Testament people. The New Testament affirms that the gospel was preached to the Old Testament saints (Rom. 1:1, 2; Gal. 3:8; Heb. 4:2).

3) The New Testament teaches that new covenant believers are grafted into and become one with the Old Testament people. It does so through a variety of images, for instance: like a branch grafted into a tree (Rom. 11:1-24), a union of two into one (Eph. 2:11-18), a brick placed into a building (Eph. 2:19-20), inclusion in a common building (Rev. 21:10, 12, 14).

4) New Testament believers are called by terms distinctly associated with the Old Testament people. Christians are called "the seed of Abraham" (Gal. 3:6-9, 29), "the circumcision" (Phil. 3:3), a "royal priesthood" (Rom. 15:16; 1 Pet. 2:9; Rev. 1:6; cp. Exod. 19:6), and "the Israel of God" (Gal. 6:16).

Biblical faith knows nothing about two holy books of divergent purposes, nor of two contrasting ethical principles, nor of two distinct peoples of God, any more than it knows of two True Gods.

Furthermore, *both* testaments are the Word of God given to man (2 Tim. 3:16-17; 2 Pet. 1:20-21). Being such, the principles and precepts contained in either testament can only be annulled or modified by God Himself (Deut. 4:2; 12:32; Ps. 119:160; Isa. 51:6; Matt. 4:4; 15:6; Rev. 22:18). Since God's Word is perfect truth (John 17:17), "the Scripture cannot be broken" (John 10:35). Principles and precepts established in the Old Testament continue into the New Testament, unless God Himself repeals them—as He does in the case of the ceremonial precepts commanding animal sacrifices (Heb. 9-10), circumcision (Gal. 5:2-3), the food laws (Acts 10:9-16), and so forth.

Having noted this, we may now consider the particular Scripture principles serving as the foundations of infant baptism.

The Principle of Family Solidarity

The Bible teaches that God establishes the family as a Creation ordinance of perpetual obligation (Gen. 1:27-28; 2:22-24; Matt. 19:4-6). That the family was of central importance in Old Testament history is evident upon the following considerations: (1) Numerous family genealogies are preserved in Scripture, thus demonstrating a concern for the preservation of family lineages (Gen. 10; Num. 1). (2) Families were considered a high and holy heritage from the Lord (Gen. 33:5; Deut. 28:1, 11; Ps. 127; 128; Isa. 8:18). (3) Responsibilities before God centered around family life (Deut. 6:4ff; Ps. 78:1-8; Prov. 13:22; 19:14). The Ten Commandments even incorporate express legislation protecting the family (Exod. 20:12, 14, 17).

Consequently, God All-merciful specifically instituted His gracious covenant in terms which included family generations as beneficiaries of the covenant, rather than in terms restricting the covenant to individuals. His mercies and blessings were particularly promised to the families of believers, as in the case of Noah (Gen. 9:9), Abraham (Gen. 17:2-7), and others (Deut. 28:4; Ps. 103:17-18; 115:13, 14). Also in keeping with this principle of family solidarity, His chastenings and curses ran in family generations (Exod. 20:5; Deut. 5:9; Hos. 9:11-17).

Godly families are thus obliged to recognize two important truths: *First*, when God's grace claims a person, God's rule extends over all that that person possesses. For example, in the law of the tithe God claims the first tenth of one's production as a sign that He has a right to all of it (Deut. 14:22; Mal. 3:10). *Second*, when God's grace claims a person, that person's household is set apart as holy unto the Lord. For example, the children of God's people were forbidden to marry non-believers "for you are a holy people to the LORD your God" (Deut. 7:1-6). Truly God keeps the family central in his gracious dealings with his covenant people.

The Old Testament Sign of the Covenant

Indisputably, circumcision was *the* sign of God's gracious covenant with His people in the Old Testament era (Gen. 17:10-14; Exod. 12:44-48). It is important that we properly understand circumcision in order to grasp the import of baptism and baptism's relationship to circumcision. Unfortunately, Christians too frequently deem circumcision a purely national and racial sign of external, non-spiritual blessings and privileges. However, circumcision was the sign of the covenant in its *deepest spiritual* meaning. Three fundamental concepts are tied up in the symbolism of circumcision.

First, circumcision was a sign of union with God. At its institution with Abraham, God says: "I will establish My covenant between Me and you and your descendants after you throughout their generations for an everlasting covenant, to be God to you and to your descendants after you. . . . And you shall be circumcised in the flesh of your foreskin; and it shall be the sign of the covenant between Me and you" (Gen. 17:7, 11).

Note carefully that God calls Himself especially and personally Abraham's God: the covenant shows God intention "to be God to you." God was not united with unbelieving people. In Amos 3:2a He says: "You only have I chosen among all the families of the earth." In Psalm 147:19-20 we read: "He declares His words to Jacob, His statutes and His ordinances to Israel. He has not dealt thus with any nation; and as for His ordinances, they have not known them. Praise the LORD!"

The very heart of God's gracious covenant was *union with God,* which appears repeatedly in the Old Testament: *I will be your God and you will be My people* (Gen. 17:7). This is a constant theme in the Old Testament, for we find it in various places: Exodus 5:2; 6:7; 29:42, 45, 46; Leviticus 11:45; 26:12, 45; Deuteronomy 4:20; 7:9; 29:14-15; 2 Samuel 7:24; Psalm 105:9; Isaiah 43:6; Jeremiah 24:7; 30:22; 31:33; 32:38; Ezekiel 11:20; 34:24; 36:28; 37:23; Hosea 1:10; and Zechariah 8:8; 13:9.

Second, circumcision was a sign of the removal of defilement. That is, it represented cleansing from sin (Isa. 52:1), for God repeatedly called upon His people to "circumcise their hearts" (Deut. 10:16; 30:6; Isa. 52:1; Jer. 4:4; 6:10; 9:25-26; Ezek. 44:7-9). Clearly then, the outward, physical cutting away of the filthy foreskin from the organ of the generation of life symbolized the inward, spiritual removal of defilement from the heart, the very center of life. Those with "uncircumcised hearts," therefore, were deserving of God's judgment (Lev. 26:41; Jer. 9:26; Acts 7:51). Of such people God commanded: "Circumcise then your heart, and stiffen your neck no more" (Deut. 10:16).

Third, circumcision was the seal of the righteousness of faith. Paul, a "Hebrew of Hebrews" (Phil. 3:5), clearly teaches this truth in Romans 4:11. There he declares of Abraham: "he received the sign of circumcision, a seal of the righteousness of the faith which he had." Circumcision was vitally related to faith. As an external sign it pictured and sealed internal faith, as the Bible clearly says.

At this point we must recall that circumcision—which represents union with God, cleansing from sin, and faith—was expressly commanded by God to be applied to *infants*: "And every male among you who is eight days old shall be circumcised throughout your generations" (Gen. 17:12; Lev. 12:3; cp. Gen. 21:4; Luke 1:59; 2:21; Acts 7:8; Phil. 3:5). Note well that the sign of God's deeply spiritual covenant, the seal of faith, was applied to infants! The family was clearly included in the outworking of God's grace to His people.

New Testament Covenantal Responsibility

Given the inspired and authoritative nature of Scripture, any principle God has ordained in His word must continue until He Himself (speaking through one of His apostles or prophets) annuls or modifies it (Deut. 4:2; 12:32; John 10:35; Rev. 22:18-19). As we enter the New Testament revelation, two facts stand out regarding the principle of *family solidarity* and *infant inclusion* in the covenant community. One is that we find no command anywhere in the New Testament—whether by implication or by express statement—that repeals this vital, centuries old, God-ordained practice. The other is that there are ample, clear evidences for the principle's continuation.

Before actually defending the above two observations, let us consider some of the implications inherent in the assumption that family generations are *excluded* from the covenant community of the New Testament era. If families were no longer considered a part of the covenant community or as partakers and beneficiaries of God's covenant, the question we must raise is: "Why?"

Would this imply that the New Covenant (instituted by Christ in Luke 22:20) is *less generous* than the Old Covenant (contrary to Gal. 3:28), thereby accounting for his excluding the family unit?

Or perhaps this suggests that the New Covenant is *less potent* (contrary to 2 Cor. 3:7-11), thus explaining its ineffectiveness where no personal, self-conscious faith exists?

Are infants of believers today *more depraved* than they were in the Old Covenant era?

Is the family of *less significance* now than then?

The answer to each of these questions must be a resounding, "No!" We may see that the New Testament clearly continues the principle of family solidarity and infant inclusion in the covenant community in that:

First, Christ treats little children and infants with covenant concern. The following passages should be read and compared: Matthew 18:1-6; 19:13-14; Mark 9:36-37; Luke 18:15-17. Let us draw a few significant observations from these texts:

1) The little children are *brought* to Him: "Then some children were brought to Him" (Matt. 19:13a; cp. Mark 10:13). They did not come on their own spiritual initiative—they were "brought" by believing parents. In fact, some of these "children" were entirely too young even to walk: "And they were bringing even their babies to Him" (Luke 18:15a).

2) When Christ states that "the kingdom of God belongs to such as these" (Luke 18:16b), He is speaking about the realm of covenantal blessings in terms of New Covenant terminology. John 3:3 and 1 Corinthians 6:10, for example, clearly employ the "kingdom of God" in this sense. Jesus is not simply declaring that adults ought to have simple faith like that illustrated by childlikeness. This is clear in that:

   a) Some of these are *infants* who were incapable of demonstrating self-conscious faith: "they were bringing even their babies to Him" (Luke 18:15a). The Greek word translated "babies" is *brephos*. According to the Arndt-Gingrich-Danker *Lexicon* it may be translated "unborn child, embryo" (Luke 1:41, 44) or "baby, infant" (Luke 2:12, 16). Luke employs a term he is quite familiar with, and which emphasizes the extremely young age of these children.

   b) Jesus is angry that the disciples are keeping these very children and infants away. He wants these little ones themselves presented to Him: "And they were bringing even their babies to Him so that He might touch them, but when the disciples saw it, they began rebuking them. But Jesus called for them, saying, 'Permit the children to come to Me, and do not hinder them, for the kingdom of God belongs to such as these. Truly I say to you, whoever does not receive the kingdom of God like a child shall not enter it at all'" (Luke 18:15-16).

c) Matthew's account does not even mention child-like faith at all: "Then some children were brought to Him so that He might lay His hands on them and pray; and the disciples rebuked them. But Jesus said, 'Let the children alone, and do not hinder them from coming to Me; for the kingdom of heaven belongs to such as these.' And after laying His hands on them, He departed from there" (Matt. 19:13-15).

3) Jesus actually performs a significant, spiritual act upon these children and calls down divine, spiritual blessings on them: "Then some children were brought to Him so that He might lay His hands on them and pray; and the disciples rebuked them. . . . And after laying His hands on them, He departed from there" (Matt. 19:13, 15). The "laying on of hands" is a deeply significant religious action. It appears in several connections in the New Testament: the ordination of deacons to office (Acts 6:6), the giving of the Holy Spirit (Acts 8:17), setting men apart for missionary activity (Acts 13:3), imparting spiritual gifts (1 Tim. 4:14; 2 Tim. 1:6), and elsewhere (Heb. 6:2). It is no mere cute ceremony.

Second, the New Testament's first post-Pentecost sermon reveals covenantal continuity. Peter expressly structures his sermon in terms of the covenant and the principle of family solidarity. Following the Pentecostal miracle of tongues-speaking, he ends his explanatory sermon saying, "Repent, and let each of you be baptized in the name of Jesus Christ for the forgiveness of your sins; and you shall receive the gift of the Holy Spirit. For the promise is for you and your children" (Acts 2:38, 39a).

Given the Jewish audience (Acts 2:14, 22, 36) steeped in 1,500 years of Old Testament covenantal thought patterns (see Acts 7), Peter quite naturally structures the promise in terms they would readily understand. Peter expressly includes their children in the promises of God in this first New Covenant sermon. Were Peter concerned that his hearers understand that the old principles are radically changed (by omitting the family unit), he certainly would not phrase this particular exhortation and promise in this manner—especially immediately upon urging the need of baptism. The principle of family solidarity is clearly operating within the New Covenant.

Third, New Testament epistles address children as "saints." The word "saint" in Greek means "one set apart" and it applies to Christians (Rom. 1:7; 1 Cor. 1:2). The salutations of the letters to Ephesus and Colassae show they are written expressly for the "saints" (Eph. 1:1; Col. 1:2). Yet in both letters Paul specifically addresses comments to "children" in those churches. For example, in Ephesians 6:1 he writes: "Children, obey your parents in the Lord; for this is right." Colossians does the same (Col. 3:20, 21). Thus, in speaking to different groups of "saints," Paul does not differentiate between children and adults in terms of their membership in the church, or between believing and unbelieving children. He includes the children of saints in the covenant community, just as he does wives (Eph. 5:22) and husbands (5:25).

Fourth, Paul teaches that children of believers are clean and holy. The child having only one believing parent is, nevertheless, set apart and distinguished from the children in unbelieving families. 1 Corinthians 7:14 reads: "For the unbelieving husband is sanctified through his wife, and the unbelieving wife is sanctified through her believing husband; for otherwise your children are unclean, but now they are holy."

We should note that Paul considers the children of a believing parent as both "holy" and "clean" in contrast to the children of unbelievers which are considered "unholy" and "unclean." Paul is working here from the Old Testament principle of family solidarity and covenantal holiness. He refers to this principle under different symbols in Romans 11:16, where he states: "If the first piece of dough be holy, the lump is also; and if the root be holy, the branches are too."

Fifth, household baptisms underscore the New Testament practice of infant baptism. Household baptism episodes are frequent enough in the New Testament to suggest the continuing principle of including infants with believing parents in the covenant. Of the twelve baptism episodes recorded in the New Testament, three are whole-house baptisms (Acts 16:15; 16:33–34; 1 Cor. 1:16).

If the New Testament actually presents a strictly individualistic emphasis in terms of the faith-community, we should wonder why only Lydia believes, while her entire household receives baptism: "And a certain woman named Lydia, from the city of Thyatira, a seller of purple fabrics, a worshiper of God, was listening; and the Lord opened her heart to respond to the things spoken by Paul. And when she and her household had been baptized . . ." (Acts 16:14, 15a). It is certainly easy enough for Luke, the writer of Acts, to specify that *all* in the family believe, for he does this in Acts 18:8: "And Crispus, the leader of the synagogue, believed in the Lord with all his household, and many of the Corinthians when they heard were believing and being baptized."

Unfortunately, many versions mistranslate Acts 16:34. For instance, the King James Version reads: "And when he had brought them into his house, he set meat before them, and rejoiced, believing in God with all his house." In a marginal reference on verse 34, the New American Standard Bible has a more accurate rendering of the phrase in question: "rejoiced greatly with his whole household, having believed in God." The New Revised Standard Version is even better: "He brought them up into the house and set food before them; and he and his entire household rejoiced that he had become a believer in God."

In Acts 16:34 the phrase "having believed in God" is a participle which is in the singular. Thus, it refers only to the jailer: the jailer believed in God; his household rejoiced. Yet the whole household is baptized (Acts 16:33). Notice, too, that Paul indiscriminately gives the promise in terms expressing the principle of family solidarity: "Believe in the Lord Jesus, and you shall be saved, you and your household" (Acts 16:31; cp. also Acts 11:14).

These five considerations concerning the New Testament record indicate the continuing principle of family solidarity before God, and the including of infants of believers in the covenant promises of God. What then precludes their receiving the sign of the covenant promises: baptism?

The Sign of the New Covenant

In the New Testament God expressly repeals circumcision as the sign of the covenant (Gal. 5:2ff; Acts 15:1-6, 24). As a blood-letting ceremony, it is not compatible with the final phase of redemption, which has its final blood-letting in Christ's death once-for-all (Heb. 10:10-12). Thus, it is replaced by a bloodless covenant sign: baptism. Baptism supplants circumcision as the sign of the covenant, for:

First, in Colossians 2:11, 12a Paul specifically relates the two rites, showing that baptism supersedes circumcision: "In Him you were also circumcised with a circumcision made without hands, in the removal of the body of the flesh by the circumcision of Christ; having been buried with Him in baptism." The participial phrase in verse 12 ("having been buried with Him in baptism") depends upon and explains the main verb in verse 11 ("you also were circumcised"). How then are we circumcised? By our baptism!

Second, both rites serve as initiations into the covenant community (i.e., the Church). In Genesis 17:9-14 (discussed above) we see circumcision as the entry rite into the covenant community (see also Exod. 12:48). The uncircumcised man is excluded from the covenant community (v. 14). In Acts 2:41 baptism serves as an introductory rite: "So then, those who had received his word were baptized; and there were added that day about three thousand souls."

Third, both rites are signs and seals of God's gracious covenant love to his people. Compare Genesis 17:9-14 with Galatians 3:27-29: "For all of you who were baptized into Christ have clothed yourselves with Christ. There is neither Jew nor Greek, there is neither slave nor free man, there is neither male nor female; for you are all one in Christ Jesus. And if you belong to Christ, then you are Abraham's offspring, heirs according to promise."

Fourth, both rites represent the same deeply spiritual truths. Remember: circumcision signifies union with God, cleansing from sin, and faith (see previous discussion). Baptism, too, symbolizes these three truths:

1) The baptismal formula reflects union with God. In Matthew 28:19 we read: "Baptizing them in the Name of the Father and the Son and the Holy Spirit." The one baptized is baptized "in" (Greek: *eis*, "into") a new family and takes upon himself a new family name, that of the Triune God. Paul teaches that baptism places us "into Christ" so that we are "in" Him as surely as we are in our clothes: "For all of you who were baptized into Christ have clothed yourselves with Christ" (Gal. 3:27).

2) Baptism signifies cleansing from sin. Note this implication when Ananias commands Paul in Acts 22:16: "Arise, and be baptized, and wash away your sins." Peter relates baptism and cleansing from sin:

"Repent, and let each of you be baptized in the name of Jesus Christ for the forgiveness of your sins" (Acts 2:38a).

3) Faith relates to baptism. Our Lord teaches in Mark 16:16: "He who has believed and has been baptized shall be saved; but he who has disbelieved shall be condemned." Luke records for us that "Crispus, the leader of the synagogue, believed in the Lord with all his household, and many of the Corinthians when they heard were believing and being baptized" (Acts 18:8).

These four perspectives on baptism demonstrate conclusively an intended, purposeful, and divinely ordained relationship between baptism and circumcision. Given the extensive arguments rehearsed above, on what grounds, then, may we exclude infants from Christian baptism? Infants of the New Covenant era have as much a right to the sign of the covenant as infants in the Old Covenant era.

Objections to Infant Baptism

Before concluding our defense of infant baptism, we will consider just briefly a few objections against it. Below are several arguments frequently urged against the practice.

Objection: "Nowhere in the New Testament do we find a clear, express command to baptize infants."

Answer: We do not deny this. But this is unnecessary in light of the unified authority of God's Word in Old and New Testaments. We should let 1,500 years of covenant history in the Old Testament receive its just weight in this regard, particularly in that the majority of the earliest Christians were Jewish and no New Testament command rescinds the principles of family solidarity and infant inclusion.

Furthermore, express commands are not the only valid ones. Good and necessary inferences are authoritative, as well. For instance, where in the New Testament do we find an explicit command to allow women to partake of the Lord's Supper? After all, at the original institution of the Supper, no women were present. Nor do we ever see women at communion. If one points to the Old Testament to show women were included in the Passover, the Reformed point for inclusion of infants is confirmed!

Objection: "Circumcision was for males only; why do Reformed Christians baptize infant females?"

Answer: Clearly, Lydia is baptized in the New Testament (Acts 16:15). In addition, good and necessary inference includes females in the administration of the covenant sign: For the New Covenant records an *expansion* of covenantal privilege. "There is neither male nor female; for you are all one in Christ Jesus" (Gal. 3:28).

Objection: "What of the many infants of covenant children who grow up to be renegades and non-believers?"

Answer: This is an unfortunate situation. However, it is not a problem solely for those who baptize infants. What of the many *adults* who are baptized yet turn out to be disgraces to the Church? Simon was baptized —although Peter soon realized he had no part in the faith (Acts 8:13, 21). The same situation prevailed in the Old Testament with circumcision (e.g., Absalom). Abuse of privilege does not annul a command of God, it simply intensifies accountability.

Objection: "Infants cannot understand the meaning of baptism."

Answer: The same protest could be urged against circumcision, which nevertheless was applied to infants. The same protest, as a matter of fact, could be lodged against Christ Himself when He laid his hands on the infants brought to Him. Cannot God include, protect, and bless even those who do not understand?

Summary and Conclusion

The case for infant baptism, then, rests upon the following lines of Biblical evidence:

First, both testaments of the Bible are equally authoritative as revelation from God to his people. The two testaments are vitally inter-related. The New Testament continues and expands upon the Old Testament.

Second, God established the family as the arena of his grace and mercy. He revealed the principle of family solidarity. For centuries of covenantal history, the seed of believers was included in God's gracious covenant and welcomed into the covenant community. They even received the sign of the covenant, just as the adult did.

Third, in the New Testament, we find no abrogation of the divinely instituted principle of family solidarity. Neither is there any word urging the exclusion of infants from the covenant community. Nor is there any instruction to the early Christian community (composed largely of covenant-oriented Jews) to withhold the sign of the covenant from their children.

Fourth, as a matter of historical fact and as theologically expected, the New Testament treats children as members of the covenant community, frames sermons in terms of the family solidarity principle, and records actions expressive of the covenant principle (i.e., household baptisms).

Fifth, baptism takes over the function of circumcision in the New Covenant era. Since circumcision (which pictured the same truths as baptism) was applied to infants, why should not baptism?

Often the Reformed Christian is put on the defensive regarding the issue of infant baptism. He is challenged to demonstrate the propriety of baptizing infants. This is unfortunate. Rather, those who neglect baptizing their infants should be urged to give just, Scripturally-verifiable cause for excluding the infants of believers from the Church and baptism.

CHAPTER THREE

Baptismal Mode

The Biblical Rationale
for Sprinkling

The controversies surrounding the sacrament of baptism have been legion in church history—especially since the Reformation and the rise of the Anabaptists. The issues regarding baptism are multi-faceted:

1) Is baptism necessary to salvation?
2) To whom is it to be administered?
3) How many times may it be administered?
4) How is it to be administered?

Over the first question, the debate has raged between the Reformed churches and their opponents, the Roman Catholic Church and various cults and sects (Campbellites, Armstrongites, Mormons). Over the second question, much polemical energy has been expended between the Reformers on the one hand and the Anabaptists on the other, and between their modern heirs, the Presbyterians and the Baptists. The third question has received exaggerated expression in the Mormon Church in their innumerable proxy baptisms. This matter also arises in fellowships such as the Baptist churches who generally re-administer baptism upon transferal of one's church membership. However, I will be considering the fourth question in this chapter.

The question of the proper mode of baptism is one to which I have been frequently obligated to respond. Having been a Presbyterian in the South, I found myself significantly outnumbered by Southern and fundamentalist Baptist churches. The baptism issue therefore does not arise as a simple question of passing interest or mere curiosity. Quite frequently the Presbyterian position on baptism has been either shrugged off as deference to tradition or anathematized as a perversion of the "clear teaching of Scripture." Therefore, the question of the mode of baptism assumes an apologetic character in defense of the Presbyterian's faithfulness to Scripture.

This chapter is not written in a confrontational or condemning vein. Rather it presents the issue in a positive light, setting forth the case for the administration of baptism by sprinkling/pouring (affusion/aspersion). The goal of this study is to provide a tool for Presbyterian and all Reformed laymen so that they might better understand their church's scriptural position. Consequently, Greek words will be transliterated and technical footnoting will be kept to a bare minimum.

The Importance of Mode

The Westminster Standards contain the doctrinal position of Presbyterian churches. These Standards are not elevated to a position of parity with the Scripture. Rather, the Confession and Catechisms represent a serious, scholarly condensation of some of the important truths of God's infallible Word. These truths were distilled from the Scriptures and organized by a large representative body of godly men long ago in the 1640s.

Through this creedal statement, Presbyterians set forth their key doctrinal beliefs in a clear and organized fashion for all to see. (See Chapter One: "Creeds and Confessions" for an explanation of the usefulness of formal doctrinal statements.) Therefore, in dealing with a Presbyterian on most important theological issues, it is a simple task to discover the Church's official position by referring to the Westminster Standards. Concerning the official position of the Presbyterian Church on the mode of baptism, the Westminster Confession of Faith states: "Dipping of the person into the water is not necessary, but baptism is rightly administered by pouring or by sprinkling" (WCF 28:3).

A query which often arises in this context is: "Is the mode of baptism important?" The answer given by the Presbyterian is in the affirmative. Mode is important. However, some caution should be urged in this regard. The manner in which one baptizes does not decide whether one is or is not faithful to Christ. Nevertheless, mode is important for at least three practical reasons:

First, Presbyterians are serious in their worship of God in "spirit and truth" (John 4:24). Innovation and creativity do not characterize the Presbyterian approach to the holy and sovereign God. If the Scriptures speak to a particular issue (especially one as important as the sacraments) they must be heeded as the infallible rule of faith and practice.

Second, we must consider the meticulous care by which God pre-scribed the Old Testament worship practices of his people (see Exod. 12 and the entire book of Leviticus, for instance). God requires that His worship be performed in accordance with His own standards. He alone determines how men are to approach Him; He does not leave man to his inventive genius in matters of worship.

Third, the very purpose underlying a sacrament is to serve as an outward, visible sign and seal of an inward, spiritual grace. Logically, therefore, a wrong symbolic picture will either defectively teach a spiritual truth (at best) or it may even distort the truth altogether (at worst).

The Issues Involved

The problem of discerning the core issues involved is manifest when we consider how divided the visible Church is over the matter. A representative sampling of churches (and cults) which allow only immersion include: all Baptists, Churches of Christ, Churches of God, Brethren, Eastern Orthodox, Jehovah's Witnesses, Mormons (Church of Jesus Christ of Latter-day Saints), Armstrongites (Worldwide Church of God), etc. However, the numerical majority of professing Christendom teaches that sprinkling/pouring are the best modes of baptism: Presbyterians, other Reformed churches, Methodists, Lutherans, Anglicans, Episcopalians, Roman Catholics, and Mennonites. Some Christian churches do not even practice baptism (or communion) at all: for example, Quakers and The Salvation Army. Therefore, key issues in the debate must be brought to light.

I have chosen to focus on three fundamental claims urged by immersionists:

1) The lexical connotation of the Greek word *baptizo*;

2) The symbolism of Christ's death, burial, and resurrection;

3) The indications that Scripture describes those being baptized as actually being immersed in and arising up from under water.

These claims represent the heart of the immersionist's system.[1] If these three assertions can be disproved, then the immersionist's argument falls to the ground.

The Meaning and Usage of *Baptizo*
Historical Development

In an article on Romans 8:29, I discussed the developmental fluidity of language.[2] Two paragraphs throw some light on the present problem under discussion as well:

> The evidence of language development is important to grammatical studies—not just in this case (i.e., "foreknowledge" problem) but throughout the New Testament as well. Language is fluid. Its constant shifts in nuance are primarily the results of changes within society due to cultural impacts from within and without, and from the effects of passing time. It is a historical fact that Christianity has greatly affected the course of history; it is only natural that this influence would carry over into language development as well.
>
> Robertson explains the historical significance of the transitions within Greek that were resultant from the rise of Christianity: "The Christian spirit put a new flavour into this vernacular koine and lifted it to a new elevation of thought and dignity of style. . . . The new and victorious spirit, which seized the best of Jew and Greek, knew how to use the Greek language with freedom and power."

The primary source for the following discussion was J. W. Dale's *Classic Baptism*.[3] Dale notes that the very ancient Greek term *baptizo* meant "dip, or immerse."[4] However, as is the case with language in flux, the passing of time caused the term to take on new connotations. This is especially true as it was adopted for religious usage. Admittedly, though new aspects of the term were added to *baptizo*, the ideas of "immerse, dip" never disappeared from the realm of possibility.

For instance, the related verb *bapto* went through the following stages of developmental accretion: First, it meant "dip," pure and simple. Secondly, since it was so frequently used as a household term, it took on the idea of "to dip into dye; to affect; dye." Thirdly, it meant simply to affect by coloring or dying in any manner—whether by dipping the cloth into the dye or by pouring the dye on the cloth. The development is quite natural and logical.

The verb "baptize" itself followed a similar pattern: First, "to merse" (Latin root). Secondly, "to merse in order to influence." For example, when a white cloth is immersed in a red dye, the action causes the white cloth to be influenced or affected by the dye. Thirdly, it came to mean to affect by any controlling influence whether in the case of dying a piece of cloth, washing clothes, defeating enemies, gathering followers, and so forth.

Though "immerse, dip" is the primary and root meaning of baptize, the idea of "influence" and "identification" are strong secondary connotations.[5] As Dale has well said: "Whatever is capable of thoroughly changing the character, state, or condition of any object, is capable of baptizing that object."[6]

This phenomenon of lexical development is not peculiar to this term alone. Many theologically significant words have followed the same pattern. Briefly note the following examples:

1) The Greek and Hebrew words for "sin" originally meant "miss the mark." For example, Judges 20:16 employs the Hebrew word *chata* to speak of men who could use a sling so well that they "did not miss the mark." It is simple to follow the growth of the term into a religiously significant word: "to sin" was to "miss the mark of God's perfection," i.e., the law (Rom. 3:23; 1 John 3:4).

2) In mundane usage, the Greek and Hebrew words for "holy" meant: "set apart, separate." It is quite clear how "holy" came to signify a state

of purity: God is "separate" from the world of iniquity (Hab. 1:13; Isa. 57:15), thus "holy."

3) The Greek word *presbuteros* meant "elder," that is, 'an old person.' It was adopted to signify an officer in the church because he was to be a man older in the faith, who is wiser and more capable of ruling in the church.

4) The Greek word for "church" meant "a called out gathering of people." But in Scripture it came to speak of the church whether locally gathered or spread throughout the world.

The various Greek lexicons give the definition of *baptizo* and cognate terms as generally: (1) "to dip, submerge," and (2) "to wash, cleanse."[7] As is evident to anyone, washing and cleansing may be performed by immersing, pouring, or sprinkling. An interesting sidelight to this issue regards the world renowned Baptist Greek scholar A. T. Robertson. It is recorded that he noted that there had been (up to his time) only eighteen worthy New Testament lexicographers and every one of them was a clergyman who practiced sprinkling/pouring.[8]

Scriptural Usage

Now the question arises: Which aspect of the various nuances of *baptizo* applies to ritual baptism in the New Testament? Exactly how is *baptizo* used in Holy Writ? As a Presbyterian and a student of Greek, I believe that two rather bold claims can be made:

1) In no place in the New Testament *must* the word *baptizo* mean "immerse." (This is not to say that there are no places where it could *possibly* mean "immerse.")

2) In *several* places in the New Testament *baptizo* (or one of its related terms) *cannot* mean "immerse." In those places it *must* be understood as a pouring or sprinkling action.

These two claims are obviously significant. If true, they in themselves would break the back of the immersionist's argument. Interestingly, two words in the Greek language exclusively signify mode: *kataduo*, which means "immerse," and *rhantizo*, which can only mean "sprinkle." However, neither of these words were employed by the Holy Spirit to denote the idea of baptism because the secondary meanings of the word "baptize" are so vital to the concept.

Hebrews 9:10

The Holy Spirit is signifying this, that the way into the holy place has not yet been disclosed, while the outer tabernacle is still standing, which is a symbol for the present time. Accordingly both gifts and sacrifices are offered which cannot make the worshiper perfect in conscience, since they relate only to food and drink and various washings, regulations for the body imposed until a time of reformation. (Heb. 9:8-10)

The word translated "washings" in verse 10 is the Greek word *baptismois* which is the plural noun form of the verb "baptize" (*baptizo*). The Epistle to the Hebrews was written to demonstrate the superiority of Christ over the Old Testament institutions and ceremonial rituals. In chapter 9, the first seven verses deal with the tabernacle and the priesthood. The priests were continually performing sacrificial rituals for sin. Verse 8 begins explaining that the tabernacle and priesthood were but shadows of the true Holy of Holies and the Great High Priest in Heaven. This being so, verse 9 explains that these acts could not really affect the conscience of the worshiper: they were prophetic previews of the final redemptive work of Christ which would actually perfect the conscience. Verse 10 says the ritual symbols were "only...food and drink and various washings (*baptismois*, 'baptisms')."

To what "baptisms" is he here referring?

If the Greek word "baptize" (and the cognate nominal form *baptismois*) must mean "immerse" as the immersionist claims, then these baptisms should have been performed by immersion. However, a close reading of the context states explicitly that these "washing-baptisms" were performed by sprinkling (*rhantizo*). Verses 13, 19, and 21 clearly define the "washings" (*baptismois*) that cannot perfect the conscience as *sprinklings* that only symbolically "cleanse the conscience." Verse 13 speaks of the *sprinkling* of the blood of goats and bulls and the ashes of a heifer (see Num. 19:17-18 for the original institution). Verse 19 mentions Moses's performing a cleansing act by *sprinkling* the people with the blood of calves and goats (Exod. 24:6-8). Also, verse 21 reiterates this same thought of ceremonial sprinkling (Lev. 8:19; 16:14). Then verse 22 again emphasizes that these sprinklings were cleansings, i.e., washings. Thus, the cleansing "baptisms" of verse 9 were performed by sprinkling.

The general conclusion regarding the lexical meaning of *baptize* is obvious: it cannot be so delimited in its scope of meaning that it is exhausted with the concept of "immersion." As a cleansing rite, sprinkling was the mode used for the "baptisms" here mentioned in Scripture.

1 Corinthians 10:1, 2

First Corinthians 10:1, 2 applies the verb "baptize" to an act which *cannot* mean "immerse":

> For I do not want you to be unaware, brethren, that our fathers were all under the cloud, and all passed through the sea; and all were baptized into Moses in the cloud and in the sea.

Israel was baptized "into Moses." The connotation of the term "baptize" here is important. In Exodus 14, where the original account is given, verses 11 and 12 relate how the people feared Pharaoh's army and cried out in anger to Moses. They claimed he had led them away from Egypt only to meet their doom and perish by the sword in the wilderness. But God miraculously intervened, parted the Red Sea, and led them safely through.

Following upon this great event, the people express a fundamentally different attitude in Exodus 14:31: "And when Israel saw the great power which the LORD had used against the Egyptians, the people feared [revered] the LORD, and they believed in the LORD and in His servant Moses." In other words: they became identified with or united with Moses in his commitment to the Lord. They became one with him in spirit. This was effected by their trustingly following him through the Red Sea: they were "baptized into Moses."

Immersion had nothing whatever to do with this statement. Exodus 14:28 clearly says that it was the Egyptians who were immersed! Israel under the influence and leadership of Moses and his God crossed the

Red Sea on dry land (Exod. 14:22). Their crossing the Red Sea is called a "baptism" by Paul. He obviously intends a baptismal identification, a union with Moses in contrast to their previous fear and distrust.

Baptism of the Holy Spirit

Another instance of the term "baptism" in Scripture which expressly militates against immersion is its usage in Holy Spirit baptism.

All Christians are baptized by one Spirit into one body (1 Cor. 12:13, cp. Rom. 8:9). The Holy Spirit enacts a vital or living union of the believer with Christ. By His redemptive work, we are spiritually identified and united with Christ and his life-giving power. When this baptismal work of the Spirit is pictured in Scripture, it is never called an "immersion" by the Spirit but rather a "pouring out" of the Spirit.

Pentecost was the initial "baptism" of the Holy Spirit. Pentecost's baptism was prophesied by Joel (Joel 2:28ff.), John the Baptist (Matt. 3:11), and Christ (Acts 1:5). In Acts 1:5, Christ says the disciples would "be baptized with the Holy Spirit not many days from now." Obviously Pentecost was in view (cf. Acts 2; 11:15, 16). At Pentecost, this spiritual event of Holy Spirit baptism was called a "pouring out" of the Holy Spirit (Acts 2:15-17, 33). Later, Peter looked back on this event and called it a "pouring" (Acts 10:44, 45).

Water baptism is frequently associated with Spirit baptism. It is the physical picture of the spiritual reality. Notice their frequent association together: Matthew 3:11; Mark 1:8; John 1:33; Acts 1:4, 5; 10:44-48; 11:15, 16. Both are called a "baptism" by use of the same term, *baptizo*. These pourings of the Spirit certainly should not be pictured by an immersion in water.[9]

Summary

The forgoing discussion demonstrates the fallacy of the immersionist argument based on the lexical connotation of the term *baptize*. As shown above, this term can mean: (1) a washing performed by sprinkling, (2) an identification or union performed by an act of trusting obedience, and (3) a pouring out of the Holy Spirit. The two-fold claim prefixing this argument is Biblically warranted and logically valid.

The Origin of Ritual Baptism

Is there any historical background to Christ's divinely ordained sacrament? Did the Lord simply create *de novo* an altogether different rite when He commanded baptism? If we can discover a historical background, then perhaps it will shed light on the mode of baptism.

At the outset of this portion of the discussion we should understand that our Lord is not given to novelty. As a matter of fact, He was concerned with fully keeping the Old Testament law. In Matthew 5:17-20, He emphatically confirmed the abiding validity of the Law of God. In the verses immediately following (Matt. 5:21-48), Christ rebuked the teaching of those who taught contrary to the Old Testament law. Contemporary religious leaders were teaching contrary to the long established Law of God, but Jesus reaffirmed it. When He quoted the Old Testament, He always said: *it stands written*, (Weymouth N.T.) or some other such confirmational statement (e.g., Matt. 4:4, 6, 7, 10). When He refuted false interpretations, emphases, additions to, or out-of-context treatments of the law, He stated: *You have heard it said*, (e.g., Matt. 5:21, 27, 33, 38, 43).

With this in mind, remember that the Lord instituted two sacraments: baptism and communion.[10] Communion is clearly the New Testament counterpart to the Passover of the Old Testament. Significantly, Christ institutes it in conjunction with the Passover meal (Mark 14:12-26). The Passover was a prophetic look at the finished work of Christ; communion is a remembering look back at that work. Also, Christ is called our "Passover" (1 Cor. 5:7). The similarities between the two are purposely obvious. Thus, we may with some confidence declare by way of analogy that there should be an Old Testament counterpart to Christian baptism. For now, however, I will let this implication stand alone; later I will comment on the precise teaching of Scripture in this regard.

Some feel that baptism is created *de novo* by John the Baptist, but this is equally a misunderstanding of the facts. The very silence of the New Testament in explaining the mode suggests that the Jews of the day were familiar with the idea of baptism. Surely the heresy-hunting Pharisees would have condemned John if he were engaging in a novel religious act. Instead, when they saw him performing baptism, they immediately thought of the Old Testament promises. They asked him if he was the Christ on this basis (John 1:25).[11] Thus, the origin of baptism surely must be rooted in the Old Testament.

When we reflect on Hebrews 9:10ff., it is obvious that the Old Testament is filled with baptismal washings. And indeed it is: Exodus 24:6-8; Leviticus 8:19; 14:4-7; 15:11; 16:14-19; Numbers 8:5-7; 19:18,19; Psalm 51:7. These are baptisms expressing symbolic cleansing. Every adult Jew would be quite familiar with these washings which were performed by sprinkling. There is only one possible exception in the Old Testament to baptismal washings performed by sprinkling: the case of Naaman the Leper in 2 Kings 5:14. However, it is by no means clear that immersion is here demanded, especially in light of the fact that all other cleansings were by sprinkling (see: John Murray, *Christian Baptism*, 13).

Additional evidence in this regard might be garnered from John 3:22-26. According to this passage, John's disciples have a controversy with some other Jews involving purification. As noted above, Old Testament washings are purifications performed by sprinkling. The controversy surrounds John's baptism. Though we cannot precisely ascertain what problem John's disciples face, it is obvious that his baptism brings to mind Old Testament purification. There must be a connection between his baptism and Old Testament baptisms, therefore. John 2:6 is evidence that the Jewish purifications are not performed by immersion. In that verse, we read of "waterpots of stone...for the Jewish custom of purification, containing twenty or thirty gallons each" (NKJV™). Few things could be immersed in this. Also, the waterpots are undoubtedly the common kind with a long, thin tapered neck to allow for pouring.

Summary

It would seem beyond dispute that the Lord employs previously sanctioned baptismal cleansings and brings them all together into the one act of Christian baptism. Though Christian baptism is not exactly the same as John's baptism, its meaning and symbolism would not be radically different.[12] Thus, it is evident that Christian baptism is not an entirely new rite. It employs Old Testament baptisms with a revitalized and fuller meaning in the light of the clearer and final revelation of God's redemption in Christ Jesus (cp. John 1:18; 14:9; Heb. 1:2; 1 Pet. 1:12). Nevertheless, the continuity undergirding the Old and New Testaments would require that the Old Testament heritage of sprinkling be preserved.

The Symbolism of Christian Baptism
The Issue

What exactly do Presbyterians teach that baptism symbolizes? In asking this question we should bear in mind a distinction between what baptism *portrays* and what it *effects*. That is, the idea that baptism is the sealing rite of the covenant of grace—God's claiming the baptized person for the visible church—will not be discussed. The present issue (mode) requires only that we consider the *symbolic representation* of the act of baptism.

In answer to the above question I would offer a two-fold reply, for water baptism has a negative and a positive aspect. First, the negative significance deals with purification or cleansing from sin. The actual cleansing is accomplished by Christ's sacrificial death being imputed to us and the Holy Spirit's regenerating activity being performed in us. Second, the positive aspect of baptism speaks of union with Christ, who is "the Way, and the Truth, and the Life" (John 14:6). This, of course, necessarily implies union and communion with the complete Trinity as well (Matt. 28:19).

Cleansing from Sin

That baptism pictures cleansing from sin may be seen from the use of three significant and pertinent analogies: (1) Analogy with Old Testament baptism in general. (2) Analogy with Old Testament circumcision in particular. (3) Analogy with the spiritual benefits of redemption especially.

Analogy with Old Testament Baptisms

That Old Testament ritual washings were called "baptisms" has already been demonstrated. Previously I showed that in Hebrews 9:10 the Greek word *baptismois* occurred in relation to the rituals of *sprinkling* with water and blood. These sprinklings represented cleansings, as is clearly seen in verses 13, 14, 22, 23. This alone should establish the fact that Old Testament baptisms are for ceremonial cleansing. However, we have further evidence.

Leviticus 14 details a ceremonial *cleansing* of a leprous person (cf. verses 2, 7, 9, 11). Leprosy is ceremonially cleansed by sprinkling (14:7, 16). Leprosy is a type of sin, as is obvious in its requiring ceremonial cleansing followed up with a sin offering (14:13) and a guilt offering (14:13, 14). The idea symbolized in the ritual is that sin needs to be removed, that removal is performed ceremonially by cleansing and this cleansing is in the form of a baptismal *sprinkling*.

Leviticus 16 deals with the law of atonement. This most serious annual, national sacrifice symbolizes cleansing as well: see verses dealing with the removal of impurity (16:16, 19), which removal is called "cleansing" (16:19, 30). This key, annual sacrifice provides cleansing from sin; this cleansing is performed typically by sprinkling the blood of the sacrifice (16:14, 15, 19).

Other passages that speak of ritual baptisms as cleansings performed by sprinkling are: Exodus 24:8; 29:16; Leviticus 7:14; Numbers 8:7; 19:18-19. These cleansings cast a prophetic glance to the future: ultimate cleansing from sin by the sprinkling of the blood of Christ.

I will deal with the New Testament counterparts shortly, but for now let us note one last reference in the Old Testament to the future cleansing. Ezekiel 36:24-26 reads: "For I will take you [the covenant people] from the nations, gather you from all the lands, and bring you into your own land. Then I will sprinkle clean water on you, and you will be clean; I will cleanse you from all your filthiness and from all your idols. Moreover, I will give you a new heart...."

The obvious reference here is to the completed salvation through the final, real atonement in the Lord Jesus Christ. His work of applying that cleansing redemption is spoken of in terms of sprinkling clean water upon the people. Thus, the Old Testament looked forward to the ministry of the Messiah in terms of His cleansing the people. And that cleansing is effected by sprinkling. This can easily be tied into the sacrament which He commands to be performed upon the nations to whom the gospel is preached: baptism (Matt. 28:19).

Analogy with Circumcision

Paul clearly relates circumcision to baptism in Colossians 2:11, 12: "And in Him you were also circumcised with a circumcision made without hands, in the removal of the body of the flesh by the circumcision of Christ; having been buried with Him in baptism." This intentional splicing of Old Testament circumcision into New Testament baptism is significant. If the two rites stand mutually related, then it should follow that they represent the same spiritual truth.

In the Old Testament, the un-circumcised man is considered unclean (Isa. 52:1). Bringing an uncircumcised person into the sanctuary profanes it (Ezek. 44:7). Physical circumcision removes an area of potential filth from the male at the very source of procreation and life. Likewise spiritual circumcision speaks of the cleansing of the heart which is naturally filthy with evil (cf. Jer. 17:9). To be holy, righteous, faithful to God's Law is to be of a cleansed, circumcised heart: Deuteronomy 10:16; 30:6; Jeremiah 4:4; 9:25, 26; Ezekiel 44:7-9.

Therefore, since circumcision pictures spiritual cleansing and re-newal, and since the New Testament substitutes baptism in the place of circumcision—by proper analogy, baptism symbolizes cleansing. The fact that baptism is once again related to the Old Testament offers additional proof of its Old Testament origin and, consequently, its Old Testament mode: sprinkling.

Analogy with Spiritual Benefits of Salvation

That baptism symbolizes salvation should be apparent to all. Salvation *was purchased by Christ's death* and applied to the elect by the Holy Spirit's activity, which is called a "washing" (1 Cor. 6:11). The Spirit's renewing power is a cleansing power: He washes the recipient of sin as He is *poured* out into the sinner's renewed life: "He saved us...according to His mercy, by the *washing* of regeneration and renewing by the Holy Spirit, whom He *poured* out upon us richly" (Tit. 3:5, 6). Scripture repeatedly refers to the Spirit's work as a pouring or sprinkling, never an immersion (see: Ps. 72:6; Isa. 32:15; 44:3; Ezek. 36:25; 39:29; Joel 2:28-29; Zech. 12:10).

In conjunction with the Spirit's cleansing is the application of the blood of Christ. This application is spoken of as a cleansing sprinkling. 1 Peter 1:2 says, "according to the foreknowledge of God the Father, by the sanctifying work of the Spirit, that you may obey Jesus Christ and be *sprinkled* with His blood." Hebrews 10:22 speaks of "having our hearts sprinkled clean from an evil conscience" which is referring to verse 19 and Christ's blood.

These two cleansing elements in salvation come to bear upon the issue of the mode of baptism. This is because water baptism and Holy Spirit baptism are associated in Scripture (see previous discussion). If the blood of Christ is "sprinkled," and if the Holy Spirit is "poured out," and if there is but "one baptism" (Eph. 4:5[13]), it should follow that water baptism would best be administered by sprinkling/pouring.

Union with Christ

The positive aspect of salvation is union with Christ. Union with Christ is a significant aspect of water baptism as we can see in the following:

First, the very term *baptizo* carries with it the idea of union or identification. This is simply a *de facto* lexical connotation of the word (see previous discussion).

Second, the formula "baptize into the name of" implies union with someone (compare with above discussion on 1 Cor. 10:1,2). The preposition "into" in the Greek is *eis* which suggests a movement "into" the name of that person.

Paul alludes to this in 1 Corinthians 1:13 where he rebukes the divisions in the Corinthian church. Some of the Corinthians are following Paul, others Apollos, others Cephas (1:12). Paul asks, "Were you baptized into the name of Paul?" (1:13). The implication is clear: they are not. Thus, they are not united with Paul but with Christ. On the basis of this identification with Christ, it is wrong for the Corinthians to act as if they are identified/united with Paul or anyone else.

In Matthew 28:19, Christ commands that believers be symbolically united by baptism "in[to] the name of the Father, the Son, and the Holy Spirit." This would be a testimony to God's claim upon the people or their union with Him.

Third, Holy Spirit baptism is the real, spiritual baptism of which water baptism is the external symbol. The water symbolizes not only cleansing but union: "For by one Spirit are we all baptized into one body" (1 Cor. 12:13). There are many varieties of gifts (12:4), ministries (12:5), effects (12:6), and people (12:12-20), but there is one Spirit who unites all of these into one body. Union with Christ is clearly taught here.

Fourth, the very sacramental act of baptism itself assumes a union with Christ. Galatians 3:27-28, NKJV™: "For as many of you as were baptized into Christ have put on Christ. There is neither...slave nor free, there is neither male nor female; for ye are all one in Christ Jesus." Those united with Him therefore are dead to sin. Union implies this very fact. The rite of baptism is the outward, visible *sign* of the Holy Spirit's true, spiritual baptism into union with Christ. This Holy Spirit baptism is called a pouring out in the New Testament: Acts 1:5; 2:15-17, 33; Titus 3:5, 6.

Immersionist's Objections to the Thesis

At the outset of this chapter, I noted that the immersionist's arguments rested upon three basic assumptions: (1) The meaning of the word *baptize*; (2) the supposed symbolism of Christ's death, burial, and resurrection; and (3) the alleged indication that the subjects of baptism in Scripture are immersed in water. These arguments will now be brought under closer scrutiny.

Claim Number One: Lexical Necessity

The Baptist claim here revolves around the lexical connotation and employment of the Greek word *baptize*. This claim was previously answered.

Claim Number Two: Symbolical Reference

This claim states that the reality of which baptism is the type or symbol is the death, burial, and resurrection of the Lord according to Romans 6:3, 4 (and Col. 2:12). This argument rests solely upon the preceding three verses with no support elsewhere in Scripture. Certainly the surface appearance of these verses might seem to buttress this argument, but a closer examination exposes the error of such.

First, by asserting that Romans 6 teaches a mode of baptism, the whole thrust of Paul's polemic is blunted. Paul's argument is forced to speak to an issue for which it was never intended. The apostle is here dealing with a serious theologico-ethical problem in the church at Rome: antinomianism. The antinomian asserts that since he is saved by grace, he is kept by grace regardless of his striving for obedience to the Law;

that is, he affords himself a license to sin since he is not under Law.

Paul asks on the basis of the teaching of grace: "Are we to continue in sin that grace might increase?" (Rom. 6:1). He answers very emphatically: "May it never be! How shall we who died to sin still live in it?" (6:2). Verse 2 stresses that the believer is actually spiritually dead to sin's power. The following verses illustrate and expand this claim. Verse 3 speaks of baptism as a sign and seal of real, vital union with Christ which is effected by regeneration (new life, resurrection from spiritual death). Baptism pictures this union with Christ in *all* of His work in our behalf. Since the baptized person is supposed to be united with Christ in all that He has done ("baptized into Christ"), therefore he has been "baptized into his death," one aspect of Christ's work.

Jay Adams illustrates the matter for us[14]: If a person is in Christ as His representative, then he is in Christ in *all* that Christ is and does—including his dying to sin. Put in parabolic terms, if a person is given ten pennies then he certainly has three pennies, does he not? A person cannot have ten pennies without having three! Likewise, if a man is in Christ in *all* of Christ in the sphere of His redemptive work, then he is in Christ in *every single part* of that redemptive work: one part of which is death to sin. The whole equals the sum of all its parts. If one has been united with the whole of Christ, he is united with Christ's death to sin. One cannot live on in sin because he is in Christ —this is the point at issue, not mode of baptism.

Second, the immersionist here claims the death, burial, and resurrection are represented by going under the water and rising up out of it. If the immersionist's picture were carried out to its full scriptural warrant, then it would be necessary for one to have his arms outstretched just as Christ's were on the cross, because verse 6 says: "the old self was *crucified* with Him." Where is the posture of crucifixion symbolized in immersion?

Third, as stated above, Paul is speaking of the work of Christ in redemption. He says that the believer actually undergoes a spiritual death, burial, and resurrection: this is regeneration. If this is to be symbolized in baptism, why is it preferred over other figures of regeneration? The Scripture speaks of regeneration under several figures:

(1) It is like crucifixion (Rom. 6:6). (2) It is like being *clothed* with Christ (Gal. 3:27). (3) It is like laying aside old clothes (Eph. 4:22-24). (4) It is like a building process (Eph. 2:22). (5) It is like being grafted into a vine (John 15:5). Are any of these aspects or figures of regeneration symbolized in immersion? Why not? Why is only burial symbolized?

Thus, immersion cannot be properly argued on the basis of symbolizing the burial of Christ. The argument based on Colossians 2:11, 12 fails on the same analysis.

Claim Number Three: Scriptural Precedent

This claim insists that the recorded accounts of actual baptisms in Scripture represent an immersion of the convert in water.

An argument of this sort rests primarily on the prepositions translated as "into" and "out of." That is, the texts speak of the baptized person as going *down into* the water and *coming up out of* the water. A frequently forwarded verse in this regard is Acts 8:38, 39 concerning Philip baptizing the eunuch: "They both went down into the water, Philip as well as the eunuch; and he baptized him. And when they came up out of the water, the Spirit of the Lord snatched Philip away." Immersionists claim that the preposition "into" proves immersion and "out of" proves emersion. But we can bring four arguments against this interpretation:

First, prepositions are seldom useful as final courts of appeal. The preposition "into" is translated from the Greek: *eis.* Abbott-Smith in his lexicon gives as possible meanings: "into, unto, to, upon, towards, for, among."[15] The function of the preposition is dependent upon many factors and must necessarily be determined by the context. *Eis* cannot be urged to prove immersion into water. As a matter of fact, in the King James Version it is translated by "into" 573 times, whereas it is translated by "to" 281 times and "unto" 207 times for a total of 488 times.[16] Obviously then, the argument insisting that baptized persons went all the way down into (and under) the water is spurious. It could just as well mean he went down "unto" or "to" the water, i.e., he went down to where the water was. Even if the word "into" were alone acceptable here it would prove nothing more than that he stepped into the water's edge.

Second, in Acts 8 *eis* occurs a total of eleven times. Only in this one verse (v. 38) do the translators render it "into." It is translated "to" in verses 3, 5, 25, 27, and 40b; "into" in verse 26; "in" in verse 16; and "at" in verse 40a. Thus, the very chapter on which the debate centers employs it predominantly to mean something *other than* "into."

Third, the preposition *ek*, "out of," is just as flexible as the other. It is translated "out of" by the King James Version 162 times, and "from" 181 times.[17] Thus, it too can indicate simple direction, i.e., the baptized one came up "from" the water's edge. No lexicographer would base an argument for mode on either of these two prepositions.

Fourth, over and above all I have written concerning the uses of the prepositions, there is here a conclusive piece of evidence that the prepositions do not demand immersion in the water. If it be urged that going down into water and coming up out of the water proves immersion, then too much has been proved. The text says: "They *both* went down into the water, *Philip as well as* the eunuch; and he baptized him. And when *they* came up out of the water." Did Philip immerse himself in the water? If the argument that the prepositions indicate immersion were accepted, then it would logically follow that Philip baptized not only the eunuch but himself as well.

Claim Number Four: Exegetical Inference

Some employ John 3:23 to emphasize that John the Baptist was baptizing by immersion. The text states that he purposely chose to minister in a particular place because of the amount of water available: "And John also was baptizing in Aenon near Salim, because there was much water there." Allegedly, he needed "much" water because he was immersing. This can be answered in the following manner:

First, "much water" is from the Greek *hudata polla*. *Hudata* is the plural form of *hudor*, water. *Polla* according to Abbott Smith means, "much, many, great."[18] Thus the translation literally reads: "Many waters." This "many waters" therefore would not be referring to one body of water but to many water sources, regardless of size.

Second, the name of the location of the "many waters" is "Aenon" which is the Hebrew word *'ayin* which means "springs."[19] Aenon is a city named for its many clear, trickling, bubbling springs. Why does John go there? Matthew 3:6, 13 tells of John's ministry at the Jordan River, which is a large source of water suitable for immersion. Why would John leave this large river in favor of a city with "many springs"?

The answer seems evident: John has a very popular ministry. As he begins preaching, he starts drawing very large crowds from all over Palestine (Matt. 3:5; Mark 1:5). These crowds need water to drink for themselves and for their animals. The Jordan River is a turbulent source of muddy water. Therefore, to facilitate the crowds, John removes to Aenon where many clean springs could readily and quickly serve the crowd's needs. Certainly these springs would not allow for immersing of large crowds of people. Though John baptized while standing *in* the water, this does not prove immersion *under* the water. After all: (1) The text does not say that he went in the water and then dipped persons *under* the water; and (2) sprinkling could have been performed while he was standing in the water (which would be more convenient than his running back and forth from the water to the shore).

Non-immersionist Counter Claims Forwarded

Before closing, it might be well to notice two brief accounts of baptism in Scripture where immersion seems to have been excluded because of sheer necessity.

Pentecost Baptisms

Acts 2:41 reveals that 3,000 persons are baptized in Jerusalem at the Pentecost celebration. It is extremely doubtful that immersion is the mode here for three basic reasons:

First, the large number of baptisms would require a great deal of time. It is more reasonable to assume they are very quickly, yet surely, baptized by sprinkling water on them with, perhaps, a branch of hyssop dipped in water. This sort of baptism might offer the fulfillment of the prophecies of Isaiah 52:15 and Ezekiel 36:25, 26 in which Christ sprinkles the nations with water.

Second, to immerse so many people would require an enormous amount of water. However, Jerusalem is not a water-blessed city: "The city was off the beaten path of the great caravan routes, and was not, as most larger world capitals, on a navigable river or on a large body of water."[20] Not only is this so, but water is scarce in all of Palestine as a whole. Cisterns are necessary to collect and store water from which the entire city drinks.[21] Especially in summer around the time of Pentecost, water is scarce. Thus, 3,000 people would have to be immersed in valued, stored water supplies in an arid land!

Third, in light of the scarcity of water, we must remember that available water would be jealously guarded. Imagine the outrage that would ensue while 3,000 followers of Christ storm the water supplies! Christ had been crucified in that very city only fifty days before as the populace cried out: *Crucify, crucify! Crucify Him! Give us Barabbas!* (John 19:6, 15; 18:40). This is the city that Jesus weeps over for rejecting Him (Matt. 23:37). The Jews would never stand for 3,000 converts away from Judaism to the despised Christ to bodily swarm their scarce water supplies in order to observe the Christian rite of initiation.

The Philippian Jailer

In Acts 16:33, Luke records the account of the conversion of the Philippian jailer. Immersion here is unlikely because: *First,* Paul is in the "inner prison" (v. 24). At the jailer's conversion, he is led from the inner prison to the jailer's house (vv. 30, 34). Evidence suggests that the jailer is an in-residence guard, i.e., his house is within the walls of the main prison. This is indicated by the language of verses 37 and 40 where Paul speaks as if he is still in the prison although he is in the jailer's house. It is unlikely that the facilities there would accommodate immersion.

Second, Paul and Silas' physical condition militates against their handling several persons for an immersion. Verse 23 notes that they are beaten with "many blows." Their wounds are so bad that the jailer, after his conversion and before his baptism, took them and washed their wounds (v. 33).

Conclusion

The purpose of this chapter is to seriously consider the mode of Christian baptism. The incentive for the study is to provide an apologetic against the disclaimers directed at the Presbyterian's position. I feel that the immersionist's arguments are not only inconclusive and unable to substantiate his dogmatic claims, but that the very proofs used for immersion can be turned around and used to defend affusion and aspersion.

It is not necessary for Presbyterians to appeal to tradition for their practice, as is often claimed by the immersionists. Holy Writ provides ample evidence to substantiate the Presbyterian mode of baptism. In closing, we must remember that Christianity is a faith that is open to all people everywhere, in every condition. All those who repent and turn to Christ should receive the baptismal seal whether they be in arid deserts or in frozen wastelands, whether terminally ill or critically injured. A universal religion should admit to a universal sealing ordinance.

Baptismal Mode and Romans 6
A Summary Statement

The Baptist claims that the way Romans 6 mentions baptism requires that we perform it by immersion:

> Or do you not know that all of us who have been baptized into Christ Jesus have been baptized into His death? Therefore we have been buried with Him through baptism into death, in order that as Christ was raised from the dead through the glory of the Father, so we too might walk in newness of life. (Rom. 6:3-4)

The Presbyterian disputes this use of Romans 6 because of the following considerations:

1) Paul is not intending to discuss baptismal mode in this passage.

2) He is actually confronting a false teaching that has arisen from the doctrine of "free grace" in salvation. Note the setting:

   a) In Romans 5:12-21 Paul shows the enormous consequences of Adam's fall: the entire human race was plunged into sin. But he also shows that as a consequence of the fall, God sent Christ to bear our sins away. He ends that section stating: "As sin reigned in death, even so grace might reign through righteousness to eternal life through Jesus Christ our Lord" (Rom. 5:21).

   b) Because of the beauty of God's gracious response to Adam's fall, some Christians at Rome (the antinomians) taught that the more we sin, the more grace we receive. Paul confronts that argument in Romans 6. He opens his treatment of the problem with: "What shall we say then? Are we to continue in sin that grace might increase?" (Rom. 6:1). He adamantly denies such a prospect: "May it never be! How shall we who died to sin still live in it?" (Rom. 6:2). He strongly urges them to quit living in that way: "Therefore do not let sin reign in your mortal body that you should obey its lusts, and do not go on presenting the members of your body to sin as instruments of unrighteousness; but present yourselves to God as those alive from the dead, and your members as instruments of righteousness to God" (Rom. 6:12-13).

3) In that the antinomians are Christians who have been baptized, in Romans 6:3-4 Paul brings in baptism to illustrate why we are not to live in sin. He notes that baptism symbolizes union with Christ. He rebukes their teaching by stating: "Or do you not know that all of us who have been baptized into Christ Jesus" (Rom. 6:3a). Union with Christ involves the believer in all the work of Christ in everything He has done for us. After all, we are "baptized into Christ"—we are not "baptized into a part of Christ" or "some of his work."

4) Since baptism symbolizes union with Christ which is effected at salvation, they should look at some of the relevant implications of union with Christ. Paul focuses on a couple of relevant implications that show death to sin and newness of life. Since baptism points to their union with Christ, and since they are united with Christ in all of His work, they are obviously united with Christ in these two elements: death and resurrection. "Or do you not know that all of us who have been baptized into Christ Jesus have been baptized into His death? Therefore we have been buried with Him through baptism into death, in order that as Christ was raised from the dead through the glory of the Father, so we too might walk in newness of life" (Rom. 6:3-4).

5) Since they are united with Him in death to sin and resurrection to newness of life, how can they argue that they can live freely in sin?

Perhaps a good illustration of the partial imagery that Paul brings to bear on the situation can be found in a foreigner's securing U. S. citizenship. When someone takes the oath of citizenship, he becomes an

American and is entitled to all the rights and privileges of citizenship (except that he cannot serve as President). A naturalized American citizen who has all the rights of citizenship could argue that he has the right to free speech and the right to free assembly—because those are two of the rights. They are not the only rights; but they are two important rights. He also has the right to freedom of religion, the right to bear arms, the right to jury trial, and so forth.

Likewise, Paul is speaking of the Christian's "citizenship" in Christ which is symbolized in baptism. Since it involves all the rights and privileges of salvation, it involves two of those rights (death to sin and newness of life) which are directly relevant to his argument against the antinomians.

Just as it would be wrong to assume the oath of U. S. citizenship gives only the rights to free speech and assembly, so it is wrong to think that union with Christ involves only death to sin and new life. So then, to limit the "oath of Christian citizenship" to symbolizing only death to sin and newness of life is mistaken. Baptism symbolizes the whole reality of salvation, not just a part. The Baptist is wrong for lifting Paul's argument out of its context, then limiting baptismal union with Christ to those two elements.

Conclusion

Contrary to those who discount baptismal sprinkling as merely continuing a Roman Catholic tradition, the Biblical evidence for it is quite strong. And the arguments for immersion are surprisingly weak.

The Presbyterian should be confident in his practice—for it is deeply rooted in Biblical imagery and exegesis. As our Confession puts it: "Dipping of the person into the water is not necessary; but Baptism is rightly administered by pouring, or sprinkling water upon the person" (WCF 28:3).

ENDNOTES

1. The first two arguments are employed by such Baptist scholars as: Abraham Booth, *Paedobaptism Examined*, vol. 1. London, 1829, 40ff. Alexander Carson, *Baptism: Its Mode and Subjects*. Grand Rapids: National Foundation for Christian Education, 1969, 19ff., 142ff. John Gill, *A Body of Divinity*. Grand Rapids: Religious Books Discount House, 1971, 909ff. A. H. Strong, *Systematic Theology*. Old Tappan, N.J.: Revell, 1910, 933ff.

2. Kenneth L. Gentry, "Romans 8:29" in *The Baptist Reformation Review*, vol. 4:2/3, 114, 115.

3. James Wilkinson Dale, *Classic Baptism: An Inquiry into the Meaning of the Word Baptizo, as Determined by the Usage of Classical Greek Writers*. Philadelphia: W. Rutter, 1867.

4. It should be borne in mind that "dip" and "immerse" do not express exactly the same action. A stick can be dipped in the water without being immersed (totally submerged) in it.

5. When an object or person "A" is strongly influenced by an object or person "B," then "A" becomes identified in that particular area of influence with "B." When the white cloth was "influenced" by the red dye, it became identified with the red dye by taking on its color characteristic. The full implications of all of this will be explicated later.

6. Dale, *Classic Baptism*, 354.

7. See for example: G. Abbott-Smith, *Manual Greek Lexicon of the New Testament*. Edinburgh: T and T Clark, 1950, 74. W. F. Arndt and F. W. Gingrich, *A Greek-English Lexicon*. Chicago: University of Chicago Press, 1957, 131. Alexander Souter, *A Pocket Lexicon of the Greek New Testament*. Oxford: Clarendon Press, 1925, 46. Joseph Thayer, *A Greek-English Lexicon*. Grand Rapids: Zondervan, 1965, 94.

8. Noted in L. S. Chafer, *Systematic Theology*, vol. 7. Dallas: Dallas Seminary Press, 1947, 37.

9. Some Old Testament verses that speak of the Spirit's work as a pouring or sprinkling are: Proverbs 1:23; Isaiah 32:15; 44:3; Ezekiel 36:25-28.

10. Arguments need not be forwarded here against the seven sacraments of Roman Catholicism or the three sacraments of footwashing groups, and other such aberrations. This would lead far outside the present scope of this chapter.

11. It is difficult to conceive of any passages other than Isaiah 52:15 and Ezekiel 36:25 to which they would have been referring. Both of these speak of the Messiah in terms of his ministry of sprinkling clean water upon the people.

12. The difference between the two baptisms would include the following: (1) The formula: John's baptism is "unto repentance" (Matt. 3:11); Christ's is "into the Trinity" (Matt. 28:19). (2) The sufficiency: converted disciples of John the Baptist are re-baptized with Christian baptism (Acts 19:3-5). (3) The initiation: Christian baptism is not initiated until after Christ's resurrection.

13. This oneness is in the sense of water baptism being the outward sign of the inward Spirit baptism. Thus, one baptism with two aspects.

14. Jay Adams, *Baptism*, 37.

15. Abbott-Smith, *Lexicon*, 133.

16. J. B. Smith, *Greek-English Concordance to the New Testament*. Scottsdale, Penn.: Herald, 1955, 105.

17. J. B. Smith, 112.

18. Abbott-Smith, *Lexicon*, 371.

19. Francis Brown, et al, *Hebrew and English Lexicon of the Old Testament*. Oxford: Oxford University Press, 1907, 745.

20. Merrill C. Tenney, ed. *Zondervan Pictorial Bible Dictionary*. Grand Rapids: Zondervan, 1967, 419.

21. Merrill C. Tenney, 487.

NOTE: Scripture quotations in Chapter Four are from the New American Standard Bible unless otherwise noted. Scripture quotations marked "NKJV™" are taken from the New King James Version®. Copyright © 1982 by Thomas Nelson, Inc. Used by permission. All rights reserved.

CHAPTER FOUR

Tongues-Speaking

The Meaning, Purpose, and Cessation of Tongues

Knowledgeable Christians are aware that a long-standing charismatic revival is all around us. The charismatic movement is so vigorous that it has become one of the most phenomenal religious movements of our time.

It is also multi-faceted, boasting a wide variety of charismatic experiences among its adherents, including prophetic utterances, miraculous healings, being "slain in the Spirit," "holy laughter," and so forth. Nevertheless, speaking in tongues (or *glossolalia*, as it is technically known) is certainly one of the most distinctive features of the movement. In this brief study, we will investigate the Scriptural data regarding three fundamental issues relating to tongues-speaking: (1) The nature of tongues, (2) the purpose (or function), of tongues, and (3) the transience of tongues. These are crucial issues for analyzing and evaluating the modern phenomenon in terms of the Biblical record.

The Nature of Tongues

In studying Biblical tongues-speaking, we must consider its nature in terms of both form and content.

The Form of Tongues in Scripture

Basically two standard positions are used to explain the Biblical form of tongues-speaking: One claims that tongues were ecstatic utterances.

These utterances were rhapsodic, incoherent, spiritual ejaculations of prayer and praise with no formal structure or linguistic genealogy discernible. Frequently adherents of this view speak of tongues as a "heavenly language." This view almost universally prevails in charismatic circles today.

The other view holds tongues were a miraculous endowment of the Holy Spirit whereby the charismatically-endowed Christian could speak a historical, foreign human language which he had never learned. Thus, tongues were a truly miraculous phenomenon of a remarkable nature.

That tongues were structured, coherent, foreign languages is evident from the Scriptural record. The following provides incontrovertible evidence in this direction.

First, the evidence from first occurrence. The definitive, first-occurrence of tongues was indisputably in the form of structured foreign languages. In Acts 2, the first historical manifestation of tongues-speaking confirms its Biblical form:

> And when this sound occurred, the multitude came together, and were bewildered, because they were each one hearing them speak in his own language. And they were amazed and marveled, saying, "Why, are not all these who are speaking Galileans? And how is it that we each hear them in our own language to which we were born? ... We hear them in our own tongues speaking of the mighty deeds of God." (Acts 2:6-8, 11)

This first occurrence is definitive of Biblical tongues, for this is the very experience prophesied by God through the prophet Joel (Joel 2:28-32; Acts 2:16-19) and by the Lord Jesus Christ (Acts 1:5).

Second, evidence from later episodes. Subsequent occurrences of tongues-speaking in Acts conform to the pattern established in Acts 2. The very next express reference to tongues is found in Acts 10:45-46 (NASB). When the Lord opens the hearts of Cornelius and his household to the truth of the gospel of Jesus Christ, they immediately exercise the identical gift: "And all the circumcised believers who had come with Peter were amazed, because the gift of the Holy Spirit had been poured out upon the Gentiles also. For they were hearing them speaking with tongues and exalting God." When this event is related to the Jerusalem Church, Peter reports that "As I began to speak, the Holy Spirit fell upon them, just as

He did upon us at the beginning. . . . If God therefore gave to them the same gift as He gave to us also after believing in the Lord Jesus Christ, who was I that I could stand in God's way?" (Acts 11:15, 17).

Note that Peter carefully defines this experience in terms of the Pentecost event. This is the "same gift"; it falls upon Cornelius's household "just as" it does upon Peter and the 120 "at the beginning." Clearly the original Pentecost tongues serve as the paradigm for later manifestations.

Third, the evidence from identical terminology. All references to tongues-speaking in Scripture employ the same basic terminology, thus indicating identity of form. The Greek word for "tongues" occurring in all instances of tongues-speaking is *glossa*. The Greek word for "speak" in every instance is *laleo*. Since tongues are not redefined elsewhere, and since all instances employ the same terminology as in Acts, and since an obvious pattern is set early in Acts, we may safely conclude that the Biblical form of tongues was constant. Tongues were foreign, human languages spoken under a miraculous movement of the Holy Spirit.

Fourth, the evidence from language analogy. The Corinthian tongues are defined in terms fully compatible with episodes in Acts. In 1 Corinthians 14:10-11, while in the course of speaking to the Corinthian abuse of tongues, Paul writes: "There are, perhaps, a great many kinds of languages in the world, and no kind is without meaning. If then I do not know the meaning of the language, I shall be to the one who speaks a barbarian, and the one who speaks will be a barbarian to me." Here we must note, *first*, that Paul *expressly asserts* that no language is *without meaning.* He is comparing tongues to world languages, and he recognizes that all languages have coherent meaning.

But, *second*, he also observes that at Corinth the gift of tongues is being employed in such a manner that no one *present* could understand the *particular foreign language* spoken. That tongues here are foreign languages is evident in that Paul compares the situation to a meeting between two foreigners. The Greek word "barbarian" indicates one who speaks a foreign language unknown by the Greek-speaking person. Foreigners do not babble incoherently; they speak structured languages—even though the one to whom they speak might not personally understand the language. This is precisely the failure of the Corinthian Christians:

they are employing their gift of tongues (languages) indiscriminately and, thus, are not benefiting the congregation any more than would a preacher speaking a sermon to them in a foreign language.

Fifth, Paul enunciates a principle which negates rhapsodic frenzy. In 1 Corinthians 14:32, Paul writes that "the spirits of prophets are subject to prophets." That is, it is not in keeping with the *Biblical* concept of spiritual gifts for one to lose control of his psychosomatic self in an emotional frenzy. In divine endowments, the Lord gifts the whole man—the rational, as well as the emotional aspects of man's being. It is only in paganism that those "gifted of the gods" lose control of themselves as their rationality is overridden by a surging of demonic power.*

Consequently, the *form* of tongues in Scripture is that of miraculously granted ability to speak in foreign human languages previously unknown to the speaker. Before moving on to other matters, though, I will survey several leading texts employed in support of the ecstatic-utterance viewpoint.

Alleged Negative Passages

Three passages are especially important in the pro-charismatic defense: 1 Corinthians 14:2, 14; 1 Corinthians 13:1; and Romans 8:26. These are all easy to explain in terms of the analysis given above.

1 Corinthians 14:2. Upon first blush, 1 Corinthians 14 seems to demand non-rational ecstatic utterances. There Paul states that "one who speaks in a tongue does not speak to men, but to God; for no one understands, but in his spirit he speaks mysteries" (v. 2), and "if I pray in a tongue, my spirit prays, but my mind is unfruitful" (v. 14). Nevertheless, these statements are fully compatible with the foreign language interpretation, as we shall see.

Please note the fallacy involved in employing these texts against the human-language position. I will begin by illustrating the matter being dealt with in verse 2. If I were to stand up in my local church and begin speaking Yiddish, no one present would understand me. Not one person in my congregation can read, speak, or understand Yiddish, thus we could

---

*Our word "enthusiasm" is derived from a compound of the Greek words *en* ("in") and *theol* ("god"). Etymologically it means "indwelt by a god," i.e., a demon.

say "no one understands" because none could comprehend my speech. Nevertheless, God knows all languages, so I would be speaking to God.

We must realize that Paul is writing to a particular church about their particular situation. As with all epistles, 1 Corinthians is an "occasional letter," that is, a letter dealing with particular historical occasions or issues. When we read, for instance, in 1 Corinthians 5:1, 2 that a public case of fornication is buffeting the church and no one mourns it, we need not conclude that this is a general principle operating in all churches. That is, that all churches have fornicators within them and a membership that does not grieve over the moral defection. Rather, we must understand that this is the situation *at Corinth*. Likewise at Corinth, tongues are being used when no one present can understand them. Paul's letter indicates serious problems with pride and division within the church (1 Cor. 1:10; 3:21; 4:7, 18; 5:6; 6:6; 11:18; 12:25; 15:31). Apparently, some are using tongues for prideful reasons rather than for corporate ministry.

Furthermore, within the very context of the discussion, Paul illustrates the problem by comparing it to a situation in which a foreign language is not understood: "Therefore, if I do not know the meaning of the language, I shall be a foreigner to him who speaks, and he who speaks will be a foreigner to me" (1 Cor. 14:11, NKJV™). Surely we may not surmise that foreign languages are not understandable *at all*; rather they are often not understood in *particular situations*. We discover an interesting parallel situation in Isaiah 33:19 where God promises future deliverance for Israel from subjugation by a foreign nation: "You will no longer see a fierce people, a people of unintelligible speech which no one comprehends." Surely this does not prove that the nation dominating Israel spoke ecstatically or by means of incoherent babble and that no one in all the world could understand their language! The statement in Isaiah means the common Israelite *present before the conquerors* could not understand their conqueror's language.

Consequently, 1 Corinthians 14:2 is not contrary in the least to the foreign-language view of tongues. We must understand this verse in terms of its original audience: it teaches that *at Corinth* those who speak in tongues are not speaking to anyone *present*—because no one present knows the language spoken.

1 Corinthians 14:14 (NKJV™). In like manner we may adequately explain verse 14, which reads: "For if I pray in a tongue, my spirit prays, but my understanding is unfruitful." Given all the previous support of the foreign-language view of tongues, we may interpretively and contextually paraphrase this verse: "If I pray in a tongue, my spirit-gift prays, but my understanding of the truths being spoken bears no fruit in others untrained in the language spoken." In fact, several modern versions lean in this direction. The Beck translation of the Bible reads: "If I pray in a strange language, my spirit prays, but my mind isn't helping anyone." The Amplified Bible reads: "For if I pray in an (unknown) tongue, my spirit (by the Holy Spirit within me) prays, but my mind is unproductive— bears no fruit and helps nobody."

Paul's statement "my spirit" refers to his spirit-gift. When he says "my mind is unfruitful" he is not saying his rational understanding lay dormant as his emotions swelled within. Rather, he means that his understanding of divine truths known by means of his spiritual endowment produces no fruit in those who hear him when he speaks in a language unknown to them. The overriding point of Paul's instruction in this context urges gifts be used *for the benefit of others* (cf. vv. 3-6, 12, 19). But if the Corinthians use tongues improperly—when no one knows the language—then they do not edify others in the church.

Interestingly, the word "fruitless" is used elsewhere in the sense of non-production of benefit for others. Note the following examples:

• **Titus 3:14** (NKJV™): "And let our people also learn to maintain good works, to meet urgent needs, that they may not be *unfruitful.*" Meeting the "urgent needs" of others is "fruitful" by implication here.

• **2 Peter 1:8** (NKJV™): "For if these things are yours and abound, you will be neither barren nor *unfruitful* in the knowledge of our Lord Jesus Christ." The "fruit" sought is in others (at least in part), as indicated in the preceding verses where Peter lists various other-oriented virtues: self-control, brotherly kindness, love.

• **Matthew 13:22** (NKJV™): "Now he who received seed among the thorns is he who hears the word, and the cares of this world and the deceitfulness of riches choke the word, and he becomes *unfruitful.*" The context deals with bearing seed, promoting the gospel among others, and so forth. Again, unfruitfulness is other-oriented.

1 Corinthians 14:16-17 (NKJV™) confirm this interpretation: "Otherwise, if you bless with the spirit, how will he who occupies the place of the uninformed say 'Amen' at your giving of thanks, since he does not understand what you say? For you indeed give thanks well, but the other is not edified." The people who hear such tongues in those contexts cannot declare "amen"—they receive no beneficial impartation of knowledge. How could they say "amen" to something they do not understand? Thus, the exercise of the spiritual gift of tongues *in such circumstances* bears no fruit—it is "unfruitful."

1 Corinthians 13:1 (NKJV™). Another passage often brought to bear on this discussion is 1 Corinthians 13:1: "Though I speak with the tongues of men and of angels, but have not love, I have become as sounding brass or a clanging cymbal." Here those who hold that tongues are ecstatic utterances argue that "tongues of angels" are set in opposition to "men's tongues," indicating a radical difference between them.

The linguistic structure of the phrase militates against the interpretation urged. The two-genitival phrase "of men" and "of angels" are both controlled by the one noun "tongues." The two types of tongues, then, are related; they are of a kind. The apparent governing relation between them seems to be that both "tongues" are tools of rational communication, either between men or between angels. They are both structured, coherent language systems.

Furthermore, a question arises in this context: On what basis are we justified in assuming angels communicate ecstatically? Surely they converse and commune in a rational way similar to men. As a matter of fact, everywhere we see angels speaking in Scripture they communicate coherently and rationally. The ecstatic utterance view of this verse is quite contrived.

Romans 8:26 (NKJV™). A final passage we will consider as contra-indicative of our position is Paul's statement in Romans 8:26: "Likewise the Spirit also helps in our weaknesses. For we do not know what we should pray for as we ought, but the Spirit Himself makes intercession for us with groanings which cannot be uttered." Charismatics often take the "groanings" here as referring to ecstatic utterances in a special prayer language generated by the Holy Spirit.

This verse is clearly misconstrued in the charismatic argument. The Greek word behind the translation "cannot be uttered" is *alaletois*. It is a compound of the privative *a-* ("no") and *laletois*, "to speak." Thus, literally the groanings are "unspeakable," "unutterable." Whatever this verse refers to, it cannot refer to anything uttered, e.g., tongues-*speaking*!

The Content of Tongues in Scripture

Probably the most misunderstood aspect of the nature of tongues—and in the nature of the case the most dangerous—is the nature of tongues relative to their *content*. Scripture is abundantly clear: *Tongues-speaking is a revelation-bearing gift.* Tongues serve as a mode of direct revelation from God to man. Tongues brought revelation from God to man just as surely as the gift of prophecy brought revelation to the prophets and apostles of old. Thus, tongues bring inspired, inerrant, absolutely authoritative communication from God to man via the Holy Spirit. Consider the following lines of evidence.

First, the initial occurrence of tongues. In Acts 2, tongues are defined as prophetic. When Peter stands up to explain the Pentecost phenomenon of tongues-speaking causing the amazement of the crowds (Acts 2:6, 12), he categorically states that the episode is *prophetic*: "But this is what was spoken by the prophet Joel: 'And it shall come to pass in the last days, says God, that I will pour out of My Spirit on all flesh; your sons and your daughters shall *prophesy*, your young men shall see visions, your old men shall dream dreams, and on My menservants and on My maidservants I will pour out My Spirit in those days; and they shall *prophesy*'" (Acts 2:16-18, NKJV™).

The Biblical concept of godly prophesying is a *speaking forth of the mind and will of God under the direct impulse of the Spirit.* The matter of prophetic claims is so significant that God's Law mandates capital punishment for false prophecy (Deut. 18:20). The claim to speak under the direct impulse and authority of God is a very serious matter.

Second, the relationship of word-gifts and tongues. Tongues are frequently tied up with and related to other revelational gifts (Acts 2; 19; 1 Cor. 13; 14). In the preceding comments above, I showed that tongues are related to "prophecy" in Acts 2. The same is true in Acts 19 where we read that the converts both speak with tongues and *prophesy*: "And when Paul had laid his hands upon them, the Holy Spirit came on them, and they began speaking with tongues and prophesied" (Acts 19:6).

For our present purposes, let us note that 1 Corinthians 13:8 unites tongues with the revelatory spiritual gifts of "knowledge" and "prophecy": "Love never fails. But whether there are prophecies, they will fail; whether there are tongues, they will cease; whether there is knowledge, it will vanish away." In 1 Corinthians 14, Paul considers tongues at great length in conjunction with prophecy. (For information on the "gift of knowledge," see: "Scripture Designates a *Terminus ad Quem*," pages 75-78.)

A difference between tongues and prophecy exists, to be sure. But they differ in formal structure, rather than content. Prophecy involves the Spirit-endowed ability to speak infallibly the will of God in one's native language. Whereas, the gift of tongues enables a speaker to infallibly declare the will of God miraculously in a language the speaker had never learned.

Third, the speaking of "mysteries." 1 Corinthians 14:2 (NKJV™) states: "For he who speaks in a tongue does not speak to men but to God, for no one understands him; however, in the spirit he speaks mysteries."

Most good Bible dictionaries define the concept of "mystery" in Scripture in terms of revelation from God. For instance, the *Zondervan Pictorial Bible Dictionary* reads: "A mystery (spoken) is thus now a revelation." The Arndt-Gingrich-Danker *Greek-English Lexicon of New Testament Greek* notes that: "Our literature uses it [mystery] to mean the secret thoughts, plans, and dispensations of God, which are hidden from human reason, as well as from all other comprehension below the divine level and, hence, must be revealed to those for whom they are intended." Bible versions clearly exhibiting this understanding of the term include: Moffatt, Amplified, Williams, Weymouth, Phillips, and Today's English Version.

Conclusion. The nature of *Biblical* tongues in terms of their form and content is precisely defined in Scripture itself. The gift of tongues in Scripture is a miraculous endowment of the Holy Spirit of God whereby the gifted are enabled to speak in a foreign language not previously known. It is not a gift of ecstatic, emotionally frenzied, incoherent rhapsody. The content of tongues is that of a revelatory message given by a direct impulse of the Spirit, the Revealer of Truth. Consequently, the message related in tongues is on par with Scriptural revelation, possessing infallibility, inerrancy, and authority. The modern phenomenon bears no relation to Biblical tongues. The modern charismatic experience, therefore, is alien to Scriptures, and is wholly devoid of Biblical warrant.

The Purpose of Tongues

In the study of Biblical phenomena, it is imperative that we seek out the underlying, compelling divine purposes motivating them. God is a God of order and design: "For God is not the author of confusion but of peace, as in all the churches of the saints" (1 Cor. 14:33, NKJV™). He operates according to His own rational decree, so that when He acts, He acts in terms of a wise plan and a holy goal.

For instance, in Jesus's choice of parabolic discourse as a teaching tool, we can discern a Biblically-defined purpose. The Lord does not speak in parable to be clever, to appear profound, or to draw crowds. Rather, He expressly informs us that the intent of His parables is to obscure the truth to the non-elect, while opening it up to the elect: "And He said to them, 'To you it has been given to know the mystery of the kingdom of God; but to those who are outside, all things come in parables, so that "Seeing they may see and not perceive, and hearing they may hear and not understand; lest they should turn and their sins be forgiven them"'" (Mark 4:11-12, NKJV™). By the same token, miracles in Holy Writ are for a particular purpose. They serve as signs from God, validating the message that they accompany, as in the case of Christ's miracles: "And truly Jesus did many other signs in the presence of His disciples, which are not written in this book; but these are written that you may believe that Jesus is the Christ, the Son of God, and that believing you may have life in His name" (John 20:30-31, NKJV™).

In like manner, tongues serve a particular divine purpose in the plan of redemption. That purpose is two-fold: (1) Tongues are a validational sign of the apostolic message serving (2) as a sign of covenant curse upon Israel for rejecting that message.

Tongues as Confirmation of the Apostolic Message

Miraculous phenomena are always attached to revelation from God. In Biblical history, eras of new, special revelation are punctuated by validating sign-miracles.

- In Exodus, God clearly endows Moses with miraculous power in order to underscore the divine origin of his message. When Moses initially balks at his task, he expresses a concern that the people might say: "The LORD has not appeared to you" (Exod. 4:1b). In response to this fear, the Lord endued him with miraculous abilities (such as the power to turn his staff into a serpent (Exod. 4:3), "that they may believe that the LORD, the God of their fathers . . . has appeared to you" (Exod. 4:5; cp. Acts 7:36-38).

- In 1 Kings when Elijah raises the widow's son from death, the widow exclaims: "Now I know that you are a man of God, and that the word of the LORD in your mouth is truth" (1 Kings 17:24).

- In Elisha's ministry, at the cleansing of Naaman from leprosy, Naaman says: "Behold now, I know that there is no God in all the earth, but in Israel" (2 Kings 5:15b).

- And the Lord Jesus Christ performs many miracles for this purpose: "Jesus answered them, 'I told you, and you do not believe; the works that I do in My Father's name, these testify of Me.'" (John 10:25; cf. John 20:30-31).

As redemptive history progresses into the post-Pentecost, new covenant era, we discover the same purpose in the miracles of the revelation-bearing apostles. The Lord confirms their message with many signs and wonders: "Then fear came upon every soul, and many wonders and signs were done through the apostles" (Acts 2:43, NKJV™). "What shall we do with these men? For the fact that a noteworthy miracle has taken place through them is apparent to all who live in Jerusalem, and we cannot deny it" (Acts 4:16).

As a matter of fact, Paul, being the late-comer to the apostolate (1 Cor. 15:8-9), draws attention to his miraculous signs as proof of his apostleship: "The signs of a true apostle were performed among you with all perseverance, by signs and wonders and miracles" (2 Cor. 12:12, cf. also Gal. 3:5; Rom. 15:17-19).

The ability to bestow miraculous gifts upon believers is itself a validational ministry of the apostles.

- In Mark 16:17, the Lord promises His disciples that "these signs will accompany those who have believed: In My name they will cast out demons, they will speak with new tongues." This assures the apostles of their authority from God.

- After Pentecost, tongues-speaking episodes occur in connection with the apostolic ministry: In Acts 10, after Peter preaches to Cornelius' household, the gift of tongues is poured out upon the converts in the presence of the apostle Peter (Acts 10:44-46). This is important because of Peter's reluctance to minister to the gentiles (Acts 10:9-16) and the Jerusalem church's alarm (Acts 11:1-3).

- In Acts 19, after Paul preaches to the disciples of John the Baptist and lays hands on them, they speak in tongues and prophesy (Acts 19:6).

- The Corinthian church is obviously filled with tongues-speakers (cf. 1 Cor. 14:26-27). This seems related in part to Paul's eighteen-month ministry among them, which provides him ample time to endow many of them with charismatic gifts (Acts 18:1, 11).

- Paul longs to visit churches and individuals in order to impart spiritual gifts to them. In Romans 1:11 he writes: "For I long to see you in order that I may impart some spiritual gift to you, that you may be established." In 2 Timothy 1:6 Paul writes: "And for this reason I remind you to kindle afresh the gift of God which is in you through the laying on of my hands."

Consequently, the bestowing of supernatural-miraculous gifts upon believers serves as a confirmation of the apostolic message. This is clearly taught in the *locus classicus* on the matter: "How shall we escape if we neglect so great a salvation? After it was at the first spoken through the Lord, it was confirmed to us by those who heard, God also testifying with them, by signs and wonders and by various miracles and by gifts of the Holy Spirit according to His own will" (Heb. 2:3, 4). It is further emphasized in the narrative of the expansion of the apostolic church in Acts: "Therefore they spent a long time there speaking boldly with reliance upon the Lord, who was testifying to the word of His grace, granting that signs and wonders be done by their hands" (Acts 14:3).

Tongues as a Sign of Covenant Curse upon Israel

Probably the least understood aspect of the function of tongues is its serving as a sign to Israel of God's covenant curse due to her unbelief. Yet Paul explicitly suggests this in 1 Corinthians 14:21-22: "In the Law it is written: 'By men of strange tongues and by the lips of strangers I will speak to this people, and even so they will not listen to Me,' says the Lord. So then tongues are for a sign, not to those who believe, but to unbelievers." To properly grasp Paul's biblico-theological intent here, I will survey some of the Old Testament's covenantal background, as well as some of the cultural and historical factors influencing the Corinthian church.

The Old Testament teaches that Israel was a special people in the sight of God. The Lord richly blessed Israel in terms of his covenant in numerous respects. He was bound in a special, covenantal love to Israel alone of all the nations (Deut. 7:6-8; Amos 3:2). Thus only they received His gracious Law (Deut. 4:10-13; Ps. 147:19, 20), His oracles (Rom. 3:2), the covenantal sign of circumcision (Rom. 3:1)—indeed, all the gracious promises and means of covenant life (Rom. 9:4, 5; Eph. 2:12).

The covenant, however, is a two-edged sword. Covenant life was one of both privilege and responsibility. Whereas covenant obedience brought spiritual and material blessings to the people, covenant disobedience brought spiritual and material curses (Deut. 28:15-68). Israel knew full well the two-fold direction of the covenant: "Now it shall come to pass, if you diligently obey the voice of the LORD your God, to observe carefully all His commandments which I command you today, that the LORD your God will set you high above all nations of the earth.... But it shall come to pass, if you do not obey the voice of the LORD your God, to observe carefully all His commandments and His statutes which I command you today, that all these curses will come upon you and overtake you" (Deut. 28:1, 15, NKJV™; cp. Deut. 30:15-19; Josh. 1:6-9). Israel voluntarily consented to the covenant (Exod. 24:3, 7) and dramatically had heaven and earth called as witness to it (Deut. 30:19; 32:1; Isa. 1-2).

Regarding tongues let us focus on one particular element of covenantal life for Israel. A vital aspect of covenant blessing for Israel is national freedom and political self-rule. The Ten Commandments begin by referring to this important truth: "I am the LORD your God, who brought you out of the land of Egypt, out of the house of slavery" (Exod. 20:2; Deut. 5:6). See also in this connection Deuteronomy 6:10-12, 20-24; 7:1-2.

Thus, one aspect of covenant curse would be the loss of national freedom and self-rule:

> Because you did not serve the LORD your God with joy and gladness of heart, for the abundance of all things, therefore you shall serve your enemies, whom the LORD will send against you, in hunger, in thirst, in nakedness, and in need of all things; and He will put a yoke of iron on your neck until He has destroyed you. The LORD will bring a nation against you from afar, from the end of the earth, as swift as the eagle flies, a nation whose language you will not understand, a nation of fierce countenance, which does not respect the elderly nor show favor to the young. (Deut. 28:47-50, NKJV™)

Israel was a nation of people accustomed to receiving signs within their covenant history: "We do not see our signs, There is no longer any prophet" (Ps. 74:9). "Then some of the scribes and Pharisees answered Him, saying, 'Teacher, we want to see a sign from You'" (Matt. 12:38). "And Thou didst bring Thy people Israel out of the land of Egypt with signs and with wonders, and with a strong hand and with an outstretched arm, and with great terror" (Jer. 32:21). "For indeed Jews ask for signs, and Greeks search for wisdom" (1 Cor. 1:22). Consequently, they were given warning signs indicating that the particular calamities befalling them were indeed the judgment of God (just as the confusion of tongues at Babel expressed the wrath of God, Gen. 11:9). The particularly poignant sign of a national curse would be the presence of a people speaking a foreign language overrunning the nation (cp. Ps. 81:5; 114:1; Ezek. 3:5):

- This sign is mentioned in the great covenant blessing and curse chapter, Deuteronomy 28. Citing Deuteronomy 28:49 again, note that: "The LORD will bring a nation against you from afar, from the end of the earth, as the eagle swoops down, a nation whose language you shall not understand" (v. 49; cp. Lev. 26:17).

- Jeremiah 5:15 warns: "'Behold, I am bringing a nation against you from afar, O house of Israel,' declares the LORD, 'It is an enduring nation, it is an ancient nation, a nation whose language you do not know, nor can you understand what they say.'"

- In rebuke of Israel's sinful dullness of hearing, Isaiah warns: "Indeed, He will speak to this people through stammering lips and a foreign tongue" (Isa. 28:11).

- In speaking of the removal of the curse and the return of covenantal blessing, the sign of curse would be removed, as Isaiah prophesies: "You will no longer see a fierce people, a people of unintelligible speech which no one comprehends, of a stammering tongue which no one understands" (Isa. 33:19).

Clearly, then, the presence of foreign tongues was a sign of curse upon Israel. And all of this is specifically related to the gift of tongues when Paul applies the sign of covenantal curse (Isa. 28:11) to the explanation of tongues:

> In the law it is written: "With men of other tongues and other lips I will speak to this people; and yet, for all that, they will not hear Me," says the Lord. Therefore tongues are for a sign, not to those who believe but to unbelievers. (1 Cor. 14:21-22a, NKJV™)

That Paul lifts this verse out of a passage dealing with covenantal curse is tremendously significant to the tongues debate. To properly grasp its import, we need to survey Isaiah's context.

In Isaiah 28, the Lord rebukes Israel, noting their priests, prophets, and rulers are corrupt drunkards whose tables are filled with vomit and who are ripe for judgment (vv. 1-8). There is no one who can understand the will of God—they are as infants in understanding (v. 9). God had taught them carefully and diligently, line upon line (v. 10); He had promised them rest and peace (v. 12a), but they would not listen (v. 12). So then, the nation will stumble and be broken (v. 13) because rather than the covenant with God, she prefers a covenant with death and Sheol (vv. 14, 15). In the very heart of this rebuke, we find the verse Paul alludes to in 1 Corinthians—the verse which gives the sign of curse: "Indeed, He will speak to this people through stammering lips and a foreign tongue" (v. 11). Sinful Israel had transgressed the covenant and had refused simple line-by-line instruction in the will of God. So their judgment is: they will no longer be spoken to by simple instruction in their native language, but in a foreign tongue by an invading nation. They would be given the sign of judgment. This, of course, refers proximately to the impending Assyrian invasion of Israel. But Paul applies its principle to the future and climactic judgment upon Israel subsequent to their rejection of Christ.

As we read the New Testament we quickly discover that Christ, "the Messenger of the Covenant" (Mal. 3:1) and the Ratifier of the New Covenant (Luke 22:20), comes to, lovingly courts, and carefully instructs Israel (Matt. 10:5,6; 15:24; 23:37). Yet Israel refuses His covenantal overtures (Matt. 21:42-45; 23:37-38; John 1:11; Rom. 9:31-32; 10:3). She utterly stumbles over Christ, the Cornerstone of Zion (Matt. 21:42-45; Acts 4:11; Rom. 9:32-33; 1 Pet. 2:7), whom the Lord had promised to send (Isa. 28:16). The generation to which Christ ministers is rapidly filling "up then the measure of the guilt of your fathers" (Matt. 23:32). Consequently, that generation (Matt. 23:36; 24:34) is to receive the fullness of God's covenantal curse: God would send the Roman armies (Luke 21:20) as "His armies" (Matt. 22:7) to raze the temple (Matt. 24:2) which the Lord had left desolate (Matt. 23:38).

Thus, the sign of judgment (foreign tongues) is given to Israel for a period of forty years between Christ's ascension and the A.D. 70 destruction of Jerusalem. God is turning from Israel to the Gentiles (Matt. 21:43; Rom. 9:24-29; 10:19-21). For forty years Israel, the favored people of God, the guardians of the oracles of God, are given the sign of covenant curse and impending judgment. The nation which had been redeemed (Exod. 14:13; 20:2) to be a kingdom of priests (Exod. 19:6) now receives the word of God from others—in a foreign tongue.

Tongues have a peculiar relevance to Jewish unbelief in this regard. In Acts 2, God attracts the attention of the Jews by tongues-speaking, after which Peter charges them with slaying the Lord of glory (vv. 22-24). The two-edged sword of curse falls upon these men, with the result that many are cut to the heart (Acts 2:37) and repent, thereby leaving apostate Judaism to become Christians (Acts 2:38-41). Peter cites and applies Joel's prophecy as indicating the coming judgment:

But this is what was spoken by the prophet Joel: "And it shall come to pass in the last days, says God, That I will pour out of My Spirit on all flesh; Your sons and your daughters shall prophesy, Your young men shall see visions, Your old men shall dream dreams. And on My menservants and on My maidservants I will pour out My Spirit in those days; And they shall prophesy. I will show wonders in heaven above, And signs in the earth beneath: Blood and fire and vapor of smoke. The sun shall be turned into darkness, And the moon into blood, Before the coming of the great and awesome day of the Lord." (Acts 2:16-20, NKJV™)

Then he warns the Jews: "Be saved from this perverse generation" (Acts 2:40b).

Tongues serve as a sign relevant largely (though not exclusively) to Jewish unbelief in the Corinthian church, as well:

First, the Corinthian church is born in a context both of strong Jewish opposition and impressive Jewish conversions. Acts 18 records that Paul's eighteen-month ministry at Corinth (v. 11) was characterized by heated opposition from Judaism. While Paul was teaching at the Corinthian synagogue, the Jews vigorously opposed the gospel message to the point of blasphemy, causing him to call down a curse upon them (v. 6). Resistance is so violent that the Lord appears to Paul in a special vision promising divine protection from harm (vv. 9-10). The Jewish zealots even pummel Sosthenes, a Christian and former leader of the synagogue, before Gallio's judgment seat (v. 17, cp. 1 Cor. 1:1). Yet despite the opposition, Sosthenes and Crispus, while leaders in the synagogue, believe in the Lord and are converted (vv. 8, 17) along with many others (v. 8).

Second, the epistle to Corinth itself refers to the Jews and their desire for signs (1 Cor. 1:22). Given the church's history, this reference to the Jewish concern for signs deserves special significance in regard to the tongues issue—which receives such prominence in the epistle (three full chapters, 1 Cor. 12-14).

Third, Paul's citation of Isaiah 28:11 is lifted out of a passage dealing with covenantal curse upon Israel:

In the law it is written: "With men of other tongues and other lips I will speak to this people; and yet, for all that, they will not hear Me," says the Lord. Therefore tongues are for a sign, not to those who believe but to unbelievers. (1 Cor. 14:21-22a, NKJV™)

The apostle is not loosely employing the verse irrespective of its true, contextual meaning. He applies the verse to the tongues issue fully in keeping with its biblico-theological setting. This is tremendously important for the Corinthian church to comprehend. For in chapter ten Paul deals at length with "our fathers" (v. 1) and their disobedience and judgment in the wilderness—and warns the Corinthians of the same predicament if they are not careful (1 Cor. 10:1-12).

In conclusion, tongues truly are "for a sign" (1 Cor. 14:22). The sign had a two-fold, yet inter-related, import: apostolic confirmation and Judaic condemnation. Tongues-speaking is a sign-gift for validating the apostles in their bringing new revelation from God. Their revelational message is, in part, that the final corner had been turned in redemptive history. Whereas, in the past God had dealt almost exclusively with the Jew, He is now-turning from Jewish exclusivism to all men (cp. Acts 1:8; 2:17, 21). The final phase of redemptive history has come, the "last days" has been entered (Acts 2:17; Heb. 1:1-2; 9:26; 1 Cor. 10:11). The Jews, who reject Christ, are about to fall under the curse of the covenant. This breaks forth in full fury in A.D. 70 when the Romans destroyed Jerusalem and the temple.

The Transience of Tongues

We must approach the question of the transience of tongues—their temporary function and ultimate cessation—Biblically and theologically, rather than experientially. In the end, we will not resolve the issue of the transience of tongues on the basis of one man's experience—or of a million men's experiences (experience does not establish truth, Matt. 7:21-23). We will resolve the question upon a "thus saith the Lord" (John 8:31-32; 17:17; Isa. 8:20). With Paul such issues ultimately boil down to this: "Let God be true, but every man be found a liar" (Rom. 3:4).

Tongues are designed to be a temporary gift to the apostolic church and has long since faded away from the Church. This can be demonstrated from at least two clear angles: (1) Their functional purpose has been fully realized, and (2) Scripture declares a specific *terminus ad quem* for their cessation.

Tongues' Functional Purpose Realized

As noted above, the functional purpose of tongues is twofold: They serve as a sign of validation for the apostolic message and as a sign of covenantal curse upon unbelieving Israel.

Concerning the validation of the apostolic ministry-message, we may draw a helpful illustrative analogy from NASA's Space Shuttle program. The launch of the Shuttle is an awe-inspiring technological accomplishment. The Shuttle is perched atop a tremendously powerful booster rocket system which lofts it into orbit. Not more than a few minutes after a majestic blast-off, after the system has reached an appropriate altitude and speed, the booster rockets fall free from the Shuttle and plunge into the ocean. Why? Why is so much technology and expense poured into the booster rockets only to have them last but a fraction of the voyage—a little more than one minute? The answer is obvious: The booster system *by design* is intended only to get the Shuttle into orbit. If they did not fall away, the entire project would be disastrously jeopardized. The boosters are designed as a temporary mechanism for the space venture.

Likewise tongues serve a functional purpose by divine design: In a sense tongues are a part of the "booster stage" of Christianity. Tongues, as a miraculous sign-gift, serve to "blast off" the New Covenant era. But once Christianity is safely on course, tongues (and other miraculous sign gifts) are no longer necessary. This analogy illustrating the temporary function of tongues is appropriate, in light of the following observations:

First, since tongues are a validational sign of the apostles in their revelation-bearing function, once the apostles pass from the historical scene their confirmatory signs would be rendered inoperative. By divine design the apostleship is, in fact, a temporary office:

1) The prerequisite for apostolic office can no longer be met. In Acts 1:22 as the apostles are choosing a successor to fill Judas's vacancy, a particular requirement for the office is stated: one must be "a witness with us of His resurrection." One who has not seen the Resurrected Lord is excluded from consideration for the apostolate. Interestingly, Paul defends his own apostleship on this very basis in 1 Corinthians 9:1, NKJV™: "Am I not an apostle?…Have not I seen Christ our Lord?"

The Lord specifically appeared to Paul to ordain him to the apostolate (Acts 9:1-19; cf. Acts 22:13-15; 26:15-20).

2) Paul informs us that he is the last apostle: "Then He appeared to James, then to all the apostles; and last of all, as it were to one untimely born, He appeared to me also" (1 Cor. 15:7-8). No apostles succeed Paul in history.

3) The apostolic office is foundational to the New Covenant phase of the Church. Ephesians 2:19-20 says: "So then you are no longer strangers and aliens, but you are fellow-citizens with the saints, and are of God's household, having been built upon the foundation of the apostles and the prophets, Christ Jesus Himself being the cornerstone." A building's foundation is laid but once, after which the superstructure may be erected for some time.

Furthermore, as a revelational gift given to confirm the apostolic message, tongues serve to provide supplementary revelation to "fill the gaps" of revelation in the rapidly expanding New Covenant phase of the Church. As the Church expands in geographical outreach, she needs a word from God to guide her. The apostles could not be everywhere (1 Cor. 4:17; Rom. 1:11-13; 2 Cor. 8:23), thus revelational gifts (tongues, prophecy, and "knowledge") bring messages from God to supplement the apostolic teaching. Once the New Testament revelation is finalized, however, such supplementation is no longer needed. The inspired writings of the apostles round out and conclude the canon and can be reproduced and circulated among the churches (cf. e.g., Acts 15:22, 30; 16:4-5; Col. 4:16; Rev. 1:3). Thus, the epistles of the New Testament are often either circular letters to various churches or apostolic responses to specific questions from a church (e.g., Col. 4:16; 1 Thess. 5:27; 1 Cor. 7:1; 12:1).

In anticipation of the closing of the New Testament canon, Jude exhorts believers "to earnestly contend for the faith once for all delivered to the saints" (Jude 3, NKJV™). Likewise, Paul can include the soon-to-be-completed body of New Testament writings with the Old Testament books by reference to the complete collection as "Scripture": "All Scripture is inspired by God and profitable" (2 Tim. 3:16). He cites Luke alongside of Deuteronomy as authoritative: "For the Scripture says, 'You shall not muzzle an ox while it treads out the grain,' and, 'The laborer is worthy of his wages'" (1 Tim. 5:18, NKJV™). The continued flow of inspired revelation is not needed after the completion of the New Testament canon. The Bible is a complete, perfectly adequate revelation from God and equips all saints with all they need for every good work (2 Tim. 3:17).

Second, since tongues serve also as a sign of covenant curse upon Israel, once God's curse upon Israel is poured out, such a sign would no longer be necessary.

In this connection, the New Testament teaches that Christ "came to His own, and those who were His own did not receive Him" (John 1:11). That is, for the several years of Christ's ministry, Israel is confronted with the gospel—but refuses it. Consequently, Jesus solemnly warns: "Therefore I say to you, the kingdom of God will be taken away from you, and be given to a nation producing the fruit of it" (Matt. 21:43). Just a few days later, the Lord weeps over Jerusalem in anticipation of the soon-coming desolation of her temple: "O Jerusalem, Jerusalem, who kills the prophets and stones those who are sent to her! How often I wanted to gather your children together, the way a hen gathers her chicks under her wings, and you were unwilling. Behold, your house is being left to you desolate!" (Matt. 23:37–38).

Israel is filling up the measure of her guilt to completion (Matt. 23:32; 1 Thess. 2:14-16), the ax having already been laid at the root (Matt. 3:10). Soon her desolation will be completed with the devastation of the temple (Matt. 24:2, 34) and Jerusalem itself by invading Roman armies (Luke 21:20, 24). History records the fulfillment of this destruction of Jerusalem in A.D. 70.

Thus the Jews stumble over Christ to their own judgment (Rom. 9:31-33). God issues a solemn covenant warning of judgment. For forty years after the ascension of Christ, tongues serve as a sign of impending divine wrath. Tongues serve their purpose right up until the end of the temple.

Scripture Designates a *Terminus Ad Quem*

1 Corinthians 13:8-10 reads: "Love never fails; but if there are gifts of prophecy, they will be done away; if there are tongues, they will cease; if there is knowledge, it will be done away. For we know in part, and we prophesy in part; but when the perfect comes, the partial will be

done away." This passage, properly understood, points to the providential completion of the New Testament canon as that which renders tongues (and other revelatory gifts) inoperative. Tongues, prophecy, and knowledge are specifically designated as having a joint terminus: each will be rendered inoperative at some future date (1 Cor. 13:8). What affects one gift, will affect all three.

Furthermore, each of the three gifts mentioned as temporary is a revelatory gift of the Spirit. Who would dispute the claim that prophecy is a revelational gift? We saw earlier in our study that tongues is revelatory. And that "knowledge" is a supernatural, revelatory gift and not merely human rationality, is clear in light of the following: (1) It is specifically designated a "spiritual gift" in its context (1 Cor. 12:28). Mundane human rationality or knowledge is not a spiritual gift for the redeemed; it is a "natural" endowment for humanity. (2) The gift is here bound up closely with tongues and prophecy, which both are revelatory. (3) To view "knowledge" here as human rationality is absurd because the context warns that "knowledge" will one day be done away with (1 Cor. 13:8d). Who would teach that in the eternal state (or whenever) there will be no rationality?

Now to the point of the transience of tongues as related in this passage, verse 9 speaks of these revelatory gifts as piecemeal—they are, by the very nature of the case, fragmented and incomplete revelations: "We know in part (Gk., *ek merous*), and we prophesy in part (Gk., *ek merous*)." The idea here is simply that during the period between Pentecost and the completion of the canon God gifts a variety of believers in various churches with these revelatory gifts. But these gifts are sporadic in that they give a revelation here and one there, but do not weave a total, complete New Testament revelatory picture. The various prophetic revelations offer at best partial insight into the will of God for the Church.

But verse 10 speaks of something coming which will contrast the piecemeal, bit-by-bit (Greek: *ek merous*) revelation of that transitional age. That which supersedes the partial and renders it inoperative is something designated as "perfect" (Gk., *to teleion*): "But when the perfect comes, the partial will be done away." It is difficult to miss the antithetic parallel between the "partial" thing and the "perfect" (complete, mature, full) thing. Since the "partial" speaks of the sporadic revelatory gifts of tongues, prophecy, and knowledge, then it would seem that the "perfect"—which supplants these—represents the perfect and full New Testament Scripture, in that modes of revelation are being contrasted. The final inscripturated word is not piecemeal—it is perfect (James 1:22-25). Thus, it equips the man of God adequately for all the tasks before him (2 Tim. 3:16-17).

This understanding of the intended parallel between piecemeal revelations and the perfect revelation is supported by the following verses. Verse 11 illustrates the matter by analogy from Paul's own physical growth. "When I was a child, I used to speak as a child, think as a child, reason as a child; when I became a man, I did away with childish things." Notice that in verse 10 the contrast is between that which is partial and that which is perfect, whereas in verse 11 the contrast is between childhood and adulthood. In verses 8 through 10 those things which demonstrate the partial state are three revelatory gifts, whereas in verse 11 he mentions three means of knowledge in the child. A purposeful parallel exists between the three-fold reference to each of the two states of partiality and childhood: Tongues are equivalent (in the analogy) to "speak as a child," knowledge to "understand as a child," and prophecy to "reason as a child."

The analogy thus presented is this: When Paul was in his childhood he thought as a child, but when he became a mature man he naturally put away childish thought modes. Similarly, when the Church was in her infancy stage, she operated by means of bit-by-bit, piecemeal revelation. But when she grew older, she operated by means of the finalized Scripture. Thus, tongues are related to the Church's means of "knowing" in her infancy stage (cp. 1 Cor. 14:19-20).

In verse 12 Paul employs another analogy to illustrate the matter: "For now we see in a mirror dimly, but then face to face; now I know in part, but then I shall know fully just as I also have been fully known." Paul here is teaching the Corinthians that "now" (Gk., *arti*, "just now, at this present moment"), before the completion and availability of the New Testament canon, they are limited to sporadic, inspired insight into the authoritative will of God. They simply do not know all that God is going to reveal yet. They are looking in a dim mirror. But when they have before them all the New Testament Scriptures, then they will be able to fully see themselves as God sees them, they will know themselves as they really are.

Thus, 1 Corinthians 13 offers important teaching regarding the transience of tongues: both by express reference and by analogy. Tongues are by design intended to serve the Church only during its inter-testamental period while the new covenant revelation is being organized.

In summary, the argument against the continuation of tongues in the Church today is two-fold: First, the gift of tongues is given for a specific dual purpose. It serves as a sign of confirmation for the apostolic message and as a sign of covenant curse upon unbelieving Israel for rejecting that message about the Messiah. As this two-fold purpose is realized in the first century, tongues were rendered inoperative. Second, the gift of tongues is given a specific *terminus ad quem* in the very passage which deals most extensively with tongues-speaking in Scripture. First Corinthians 13 teaches that all partial revelational modes are supplanted by the perfect, final revelation—the completed word of God.

Conclusion

Much more needs to be said regarding the modern tongues phenomenon. These three issues, however, are certainly among the more crucial matters for grasping the import of tongues in redemptive history. The exegetical evidence is clear: Tongues were miraculous endowments of foreign language bringing inspired revelation from God to the first century Church and warning to the Jews of the judgment to befall them in A.D. 70. Tongues served an important—though temporary—function in their time. Biblical tongues no longer exist. Those Christians who experience tongues-speaking are either (1) simply caught up in their enthusiasm for God and allowing their emotions to run away with them, or (2) have learned their conduct from their worship community.

NOTE: Scripture quotations are from the New American Standard Bible unless otherwise noted. Scripture quotations marked "NKJV™" are taken from the New King James Version®. Copyright © 1982 by Thomas Nelson, Inc. Used by permission. All rights reserved.

Doctrinal Issues

NOTE: Scripture quotations are from the New American Standard Bible unless otherwise noted. Scripture quotations marked "NKJV™" are taken from the New King James Version®. Copyright © 1982 by Thomas Nelson, Inc. Used by permission. All rights reserved.

CHAPTER FIVE

Defending the Faith

An Introduction to Biblical Apologetics

God calls upon Christians to "sanctify the Lord God in your hearts, and always be ready to give a defense to everyone who asks you a reason for the hope that is in you, with meekness and fear" (1 Pet. 3:15, NKJV™). As we obey Him, we must defend the faith in such a way that it "sanctifies the Lord" in our hearts. We must defend the faith from a position of faith. Too many defenses of the faith cede the method of approach to the unbeliever and end up "proving" at best the *possibility* that *a god* exists—not the *certainty* that the God of Scripture exists.

Let us see how we may do this.

The Role of Presuppositions in Thought

The Uniformity of Nature and Thought

We exist in what is known as a "universe." The word "universe" is composed of two Latin parts: "uni" (from *unus* meaning "one," as in "unit") and "verse" (from *vertere*, meaning "turn"). It speaks of all created things regarded collectively. This word indicates that we live in a *single* unified and orderly system which is composed of many diversified parts. These parts function coordinately together as a whole, rational system. We do not live in a "multiverse." A multiverse state-of-affairs would be a dis-unified, totally fragmented, and random assortment of disconnected and un*connectable* facts. These unconnectable facts would be meaning-lessly scattered about in chaotic disarray and ultimate disorder.

The concept of a *universe* is vitally important to science, since the very possibility of scientific investigation is totally dependent upon the fact of a "*uni*-verse"—an orderly, rational coherent, unified system. If it were the case that reality were haphazard and disorderly, there could be no basic scientific laws that govern and control various phenomena. And if this were so there could be no unity at all in either reality itself, or in experience, or in thought.

In such a multiverse each and every single fact would necessarily stand alone, utterly disconnected from other facts, not forming a system as a whole. Consequently, nothing could be organized and related in a mind because no fact would be related to any other fact. Thus, science, logic, and experience are absolutely dependent upon uniformity as a principle of the natural world.

Uniformity and Faith

But now the question arises: How do we know assuredly that the universe is in fact uniform? Has man investigated every single aspect of the universe from each one of its smallest atomic particles to the farthest corners of its galaxies—and all that exists in between—so that he can speak authoritatively? Does man have totally exhaustive knowledge about every particle of matter, every movement in space, and every moment of time? How does man know uniformity governs the world and the universe? Furthermore, how can we know that uniformity will continue tomorrow so that we can conjecture about future events? And since man claims to have an experience of external things, how do we know our experience is accurate and actually conforms to reality as it is?

Such questions are not commonly asked but are, nevertheless, vitally important to consider. The point of these questions is to demonstrate a particular phenomenon: we must realize that any and every attempt to prove uniformity in nature necessarily requires *circular reasoning*. To prove uniformity one must assume or presuppose uniformity.

If I set out to argue the uniformity of the universe because I can pre-dict cause-and-effect, am I not presupposing the uniformity and validity of my experience? How can I be sure that my experience of cause and effect is an accurate reflection of what really happens? Furthermore, am I not presupposing the trustworthy, uniform coherence of my own rationality—a rationality that requires uniformity?

The issue boils down to this: Since man cannot know everything he must *assume* or *presuppose* uniformity and then think and act on this very basic assumption. *Consequently, the principle of uniformity is not a scientific law but an act of faith which undergirds scientific law.* Thus, adherence to the principle of uniformity—though basic to science—is an intrinsically religious commitment.

Presuppositions in Thought

Scientists follow a basic pattern in discovering true scientific laws. First, they observe a particular phenomenon. Then, on the basis of their observations, they construct a working hypothesis. Next, experiments are performed implementing this hypothesis. This is followed in turn by an attempt to verify the experiments performed. Then a verified hypothesis is accepted as a theory. Finally a well-established theory is recognized as a scientific law which governs in a given set of circumstances.

Thus, the basic pattern of scientific activity is: observation, hypothesis, experimentation, verification, theory, and law. Christians agree wholeheartedly with the validity of this scientific methodology. We accept the notion of a uniform universe which allows for such, for "in the beginning God created the heavens and the earth" (Gen. 1:1).

Physicist Thomas Kuhn, in his epochal 1962 work titled *The Structure of Scientific Revolutions*, noted that scientists *must* work from certain *preconceived* ideas, certain *presupposed* concepts about things in order to begin formulating their theories and performing their experiments. That presuppositions are always silently at work is evident in that when dealing with a particular problem, scientists select only a few basic facts to consider while rejecting or overlooking numerous others. They perform certain types of experiments while neglecting others. *And they do this in keeping with their presuppositions.* One of the most basic presuppositions held by scientists is the one we have been considering: the universe is in fact one orderly, logical, coherent system.

Were this not assumed then science could not even get off the ground.

But, as a matter of fact, there are *numerous* presuppositions that all men hold that play a vital role in all human thought and behavior. The various presuppositions we hold govern the way we think and act all the way down to how we select and employ specific facts from the countless number presented to us each moment. Basic presuppositions are the foundation blocks upon which we build our way of understanding the world about us. Presuppositions are the very basis for what is known as our "world-and-life" view.

A world-and-life view is the framework through which we understand the world and our relation to it. Everyone necessarily has a particular way of looking at the world which serves to organize ideas about the world in his mind. This world-and-life view must be founded on basic presupposed ideas that we hold to be truth. We begin with certain presuppositions and build from there in our learning, communicating, behaving, planning, and so forth.

The Impossibility of Neutrality

Everyone holds to presuppositions. No one operates—or even *can* operate—from a vacuum. We simply do not think or behave "out of the blue." It is impossible to think and live as if we were aliens having just arrived in this world from a radically different universe, totally devoid of all knowledge of this world, absolutely objective and utterly unpredisposed to ideas about truth: People behave in terms of a basic world-and-life view which implements their conceptions regarding truth.

Consequently, neutrality in thought is impossible. Each person—the philosopher and scientist included—has his own bias. This bias has predetermined the *facts* on the basis of his presuppositions. Yet almost invariably scientists claim to be presenting neutral, unbiased, impartial, and objective facts in their research. But man is not and cannot be truly objective and impartial. *All thinking must begin somewhere!* All thinking must have some fundamental, logically primitive starting point or presupposition. At the very least, we must presuppose the reality of the external world, the rationality of mental activity, the compatibility between external reality and the mind, and the uniformity of nature, i.e., the law of cause and effect. As noted previously, a certain *faith* is necessary in the selection and organization of the several facts chosen from the innumerable number flowing toward us in every moment of experience. By the very nature of the case, *presuppositions are necessarily self-authenticating or self-evidencing.* Facts are inseparable from their interpretation. Facts *cannot* stand alone. They must be understood in terms of some broad, unified whole or system. They must be organized in our rational minds in terms of their general relationships to other facts and principles.

This leads us, then, to our most basic question: Which system of thought can give meaning to the facts of the universe? Which world-and-life view can provide an adequate foundation for reality? Why is our state of affairs conducive to rational thought and behavior? What is the basis for an orderly universe?

Worldviews in Collision

When we contrast Christian thought with non-Christian thought, we must realize that we are *not* contrasting two series of isolated facts. We are not comparing two systems of truth sharing a basically similar outlook with only intermittent differences at specific turns. *We are contrasting two whole, complete, and antithetical systems of thought.* Each particular item of evidence presented in support of the one system will be evaluated by the other system in terms of the latter's own entire implicit *system* with all of its basic assumptions. Each fact or piece of data presented either to the Christian or the non-Christian will be weighed, categorized, organized, and judged as to its possibility and significance in terms of the all pervasive world-and-life view held.

Consequently, it is essential that we see the debate between the Christian and the non-Christian as between two complete world-and-life views—between two ultimate commitments and presuppositions which are contrary to one another. Two complete philosophies are in collision. Appealing to various *scientific evidences* would be arbitrated *in terms of* the two mutually-exclusive and diametrically opposed, presupposed truths held by the systems.

Thus, the debate between the Christian and the non-Christian *must eventually work its way down to the question of one's ultimate authority.*

Every series of arguments must end somewhere; one's conclusions could never be demonstrated if they were dependent upon an infinite regress of argumentation and justification. So all debates must terminate at *some* point, at some premise held as unquestionable. This is one's foundational starting point, one's ultimate authority or presupposition.

The question which surfaces at this point is this: Which system of truth provides the foundational preconditions essential for observation, reason, experience, and meaningful discourse? Thus, which *faith* system should be chosen; the Christian or the non-Christian?

The Christian System and Presuppositions

What is the Christian's starting point? What is his most basic presupposition upon which he builds his entire world-and-life view? Where do we begin our argument?

Christian thought holds as its logically primitive, fundamental, all-pervasive, and necessary starting point or presupposition, the being of God who has revealed Himself in Scripture. Thus, our presupposition is God and His word. The Scripture, being His own infallible word (2 Tim. 3:16), reveals to us the nature of the God in Whom we trust.

God is self-sufficient, needing nothing outside of Himself at all (Exod. 4:11; John 5:26). All else in the universe is utterly dependent upon Him (Col. 1:17; Heb. 1:3). God is the all-powerful Creator of the entire universe (Gen. 1:1; Exod. 20:11; Neh. 9:6). God is personal, thus giving meaning to the vast universe (Acts 17:28). And God has clearly and authoritatively revealed Himself in Scripture (2 Pet. 1:20-21), so we may build upon His word as Truth (Ps. 119:160; John 17:17).

The entire Christian system of thought is founded solidly upon this God; the all-ordering God of Scripture (Ps. 33:9; Isa. 46:10). We presuppose God for what He is. If God exists and demands our belief in Scripture, we cannot challenge or test Him in any area (Deut. 6:16; Matt. 4:7). We recognize the independence of God and the utter dependence of man and the universe. Thus we do not have to exhaustively know everything to be sure. God knows all things and has revealed to us in His word the truth of uniformity (Gen. 8:22; Col. 1:17; Heb. 1:3) and all other truths we need to build upon.

The Non-Christian System and Presuppositions

Against this presupposed system, what does the non-Christian presuppose as ultimate truth? What does the secularist have to offer as its ultimate authority?

The non-Christian must ultimately explain the universe *not* on the basis of the all-organizing, self-sufficient, all-wise, personal God as his starting point, but rather by nebulous, chaotic, impersonal chance. He asserts that the universe was produced by a combination of impersonal chance plus an enormous span of time. Thus the ultimate starting point and the all-conditioning environment of the universe is *time plus chance*. Consequently, *rational* science is rooted in the *irrationality* of chance. The scientist cannot speak of design or purpose in the universe because there is no designer or purpose. There can be no goal or purpose in a random system.

On this view, science *must* by the very nature of its non-Christian commitment assume facts to be bits of irrationalism strewn about awaiting rationalization by man. Thus modem science is schizophrenic. On the one hand, everything has its source in random, ungoverned chance. On the other hand, evolution assumes all is not random, but uniform: that all is ungoverned, yet, nevertheless, is moving in an upward direction from disorder to order, from simplicity to complexity.

In this regard, Christian apologist Cornelius Van Til has noted: "On his own assumption, his own rationality is a product of chance. The rationality and purpose that he may be searching for are still bound by products of chance." To prove a rational universe by chance, man must believe the rational is the product of, and is dependent upon, the irrational.

Not only is all of reality founded on chance, but this leaves man to be the final criterion of truth, Man—sinful, fallible, finite man—becomes ultimate in the non-Christian system.

Presuppositions Make a Difference

Reality (*Ontology*)

When asked to give the basis and starting point for the orderly universe and all external reality, the Christian points to the self-contained, omnipresent all-powerful, all-wise God of Scripture.

When the non-Christian is asked to give the basis and starting for the orderly universe and external reality, he points, literally, to nothing. All has risen from nothing by the irrational mechanism of chance. When asked if something can miraculously pop into being from nothing in an instant, the non-Christian vigorously responds in the negative. Instant miracles are out of the question! But when asked if something can come out of nothing *if given several billion years*, the non-Christian confidently responds in the affirmative. As Van Til has noted, the non-Christian overlooks the fact that if one zero equals zero, then a billion zeros can equal only zero.

Thus, the Christian has a *more than adequate reason* for the universe, whereas the non-Christian has *no reason whatsoever*.

Knowledge (*Epistemology*)

The Christian establishes his theory of knowledge on the all-ordering omniscient God of Scripture. God has instantaneous, true, and exhaustive knowledge of everything. And He has revealed to man in the Bible comprehensive principles which are clear and give a sure foundation for knowledge. Such a foundation ensures that what man does know (although he cannot know all things), he can know truly. Knowledge does work because man's mind as created by God is receptive to external reality and is given validity by God Himself.

On the other hand, the non-Christian must establish his theory of knowledge on the same foundation upon which he established reality: nebulous chaos and irrational chance. If followed out consistently, the non-Christian theory of knowledge would utterly destroy all knowledge, causing it to drown in the turbulent ocean of irrationalism. *There is no reason for reason in the non-Christian system.* The concepts of probability, possibility, order, rationality, and so forth, are impossible in a chance system.

Thus, the Christian has a sure foundation for knowledge, whereas the non-Christian has none.

Ethics (*Morality*)

When we consider the issue of moral behavior—how we shall conduct ourselves—again, the question must be settled in terms of one's system.

For the Christian, morality is founded upon the all-good, all-knowing, everywhere present, all-powerful, personal, and eternal God of Scripture. His will, which is rooted in His being and nature, is man's standard of right. Since God is all good (Ps. 119:137; Mark 10:18b) and all-knowing (Ps. 139:2-24; Prov. 15:3), moral principles revealed in Scripture are always relevant to our situation. Since God is eternal (Ps. 90:2; 102:12), His moral commands are *always* binding upon men.

For the non-Christian there is no sure base for ethics. Since reality is founded on nothing and knowledge is rooted in irrationalism, morality can be nothing other than pure, impersonal irrelevance. In such a system as presupposed by non-Christian thought, there are no—*there can be no* —ultimate, abiding moral principles. Everything is caught up in the impersonal flux of a random universe. Random change is an ultimate in such a system, consequently, ethics is reduced to pure relativism. Non-Christian thought can offer no justification for any moral behavior whatsoever.

Purpose (*Teleology*)

To the question of whether or not there is *any* significance and meaning to the universe and to life, the Christian confidently responds in the affirmative. There is meaning in the world because it was purposely and purposefully created by and for the personal, loving, all-ordering, eternal God of Scripture (Neh. 9:6; Ps. 33:6-9). Man came about as the direct and purposeful creation of the loving God (Gen. 2:7). Furthermore, man was assigned a specific and far-reaching duty by God on the very day he was created (Gen. 1:26-29). Man and *his task* must be understood *in terms of* the eternal God and His plan rather than *in terms of* himself and an environment of chance and change.

Non-Christian thought destroys the meaning and significance of man by positing that he is nothing more than a chance fluke, an accidental collection of molecules arising out of the slime and primordial ooze. Man is a frail speck of dust caught up in a gigantic, impersonal, multi-billion-year-old universe. That, and nothing more. As the famous twentieth century atheist Bertrand Russell put it:

> The world is purposeless, void of meaning. Man is the outcome of accidental collocations of atoms; all the devotion, all the

inspiration, all the noonday brightness of human genius are destined to extinction in the vast death of the solar system. Only on the firm foundation of unyielding despair can the soul's habitation be safely built. From evolution, no ultimately optimistic philosophy can be validly inferred. (Russell, *Mysticism and Logic.* New York: Doubleday, 1917, 45-46)

Conclusion

To the question concerning which system is the most adequate to explain external reality, the possibility of knowledge, a relevant and binding ethic, and the significance of man, the answer should be obvious. Actually, the defense of Christianity is simple: we argue the impossibility of the contrary. Those who assault the Christian system must actually *assume* the Christian system to do so. In fact, atheism assumes theism. If the God of Scripture did not exist, there would be no man in any real world to argue—there would be no possibility of rationality by which an argument could be forged, and there would be no purpose in debate!

Charles Darwin stated it well in his personal letter to W. Graham on July 3, 1881:

> But then with me the horrid doubt always arises whether the convictions of man's mind, which has always been developed from the mind of the lower animals, are of any value or at all trustworthy. Would any one trust in the convictions of a monkey's mind, if there are any convictions in such a mind? (Francis Darwin, ed., *The Life and Letters of Charles Darwin.* New York: Basic, 1959, 1:285)

Paul also spoke well when he declared in Romans 3:4 (NKJV™), "Let God be true but every man a liar."

The God of Scripture, the Father of our Lord Jesus Christ is the ultimate and necessary foundation for a rational, coherent worldview. Every other system is built upon a lie. The Christian system begins with: "In the beginning God." And from that foundational reality, all the rest of a rational worldview falls into place.

CHAPTER SIX

Six Day Creation

A Defense of the
Traditional Exegesis

The great reformer John Calvin asserted that "God Himself took the space of six days" to create the world (*Genesis*, at 1:5). Our church's Confession agrees, declaring that God created the world "in the space of six days" (WCF 4:1). But recently this clear temporal affirmation based on the opening narrative of God's Word has been radically re-interpreted by some reformed theologians. Was Calvin correct? The divines? Did they "accurately handle" the word of God? Or were they naive children of their times?

In this chapter, I will introduce several compelling reasons for interpreting the days of Genesis 1 in a straightforward manner that demands both their *chronological succession* and *twenty-four-hour duration*. Then I will briefly consider common objections to the traditional exegesis.

The Argument for Literal, Chronological Days

1. *Argument from Primary Meaning*

The preponderant usage of the word "day" (Heb. *yom*) in the Old Testament is of a normal diurnal period. The overwhelming majority of its 2,304 appearances in the Old Testament clearly refer either to a normal, full day-and-night cycle, or to the lighted portion of that cycle. In fact, on Day One God Himself "called" the light "day" (Gen. 1:5), establishing the temporal significance of the term in the creation week. As Berkhof declares in defending a six-day creation: "In its primary meaning, the word *yom* denotes a natural day; and it is a good rule in exegesis, not to depart from the primary meaning of a word, unless this is required by the context" (*Systematic Theology*, 154).

2. Argument from Explicit Qualification

So that we not miss his point, Moses relentlessly qualifies each of the six creation days by "evening and morning." Outside of Genesis 1 the words "evening" and "morning" appear in statements thirty-two times in the Old Testament, presenting the two parts defining a normal day (e.g., Exod. 16:13; 18:13; 27:21). Robert L. Dabney observed in defending a six-day creation: "The sacred writer seems to shut us up to the literal interpretation by describing the days as comprised of its natural parts, morning and evening" (*Systematic Theology*, 255).

3. Argument from Numerical Prefix

Genesis 1 attaches a numeral to each of the creation days: first, second, third, etc. Moses affixes numerical adjectives to *yom* 119 times in his writings. These always signify literal days, as in circumcision on the "eighth day" (Lev. 12:3; cp. Num. 33:38). The same holds true for the 357 times numerical adjectives qualify *yom* outside the Pentateuch. (Hosea 6:2 is no counter example. It either refers to the certainty of Israel's national resurrection, using the literal time period at which a body begins to decompose [John 11:39] to underscore their hope. Or it may be alluding to Christ's resurrection on the third day as Israel's hope [1 Cor. 15:4].) As Gerhard Hasel observes: "This triple interlocking connection of singular usage, joined by a numeral, and the temporal definition of 'evening and morning,' keeps the creation 'day' the same throughout the creation account. It also reveals that time is conceived as linear and events occur within it successively. To depart from the numerical, consecutive linkage and the 'evening-morning' boundaries in such direct language would mean to take extreme liberty with the plain and direct meaning of the Hebrew language" ("The 'Days' of Creation," *Origins* 21:1, 1984, 26).

4. Argument from Numbered Series

In a related though slightly different observation, we note that when *yom* appears in numbered series it always specifies natural days (e.g., Exod. 12:15-16; 24:16; Lev. 23:39; Num. 7:12-36; 29:17ff.). Genesis 1 has a series of consecutively numbered days for a reason: to indicate sequentially flowing calendrical days. As E. J. Young observes over against the Framework view: "If Moses had intended to teach a non-chronological view of the days, it is indeed strange that he went out of his way, as it were, to emphasize chronology and sequence.... It is questionable whether serious exegesis of Genesis 1 would in itself lead anyone to adopt a non-chronological view of the days for the simple reason that everything in the text militates against it" (Young, *Genesis One*, 100). Derek Kidner agrees: "The march of the days is too majestic a progress to carry no implication of ordered sequence; it also seems over-subtle to adopt a view of the passage which discounts one of the primary impressions it makes on the ordinary reader" (*Genesis*, 54-55). Wayne Grudem concurs: "The implication of chronological sequence in the narrative is almost inescapable" (*Systematic Theology*, 303).

5. Argument from Coherent Usage

The word *yom* in Genesis 1 defines Days 4 to 6—*after* God creates the sun expressly for marking off days (Gen. 1:14, 18). Interestingly, Moses emphasizes Day 4 by allocating the second greatest number of words to describe it. Surely these last three days of creation are normal days. Yet nothing in the text suggests a change of temporal function for *yom* from the first three days: they are measured by the same temporal designator (*yom*), along with the same qualifiers (numerical adjectives and "evening and morning"). Should not Days 1 to 3 demarcate normal days also?

6. Argument from Divine Exemplar

The Scripture specifically patterns man's work week after God's own original creation week (Exod. 20:9-11; 31:17). And as stated there, such is not for purposes of analogy, but imitation. Besides, to *what* could the creation days be analogous? God dwells in timeless eternity (Isa. 57:15) and does not exist under temporal constraints (2 Pet. 3:8). Irons states that: "God has not chosen to reveal that information" (Irons, "The Framework Interpretation Explained and Defended," [1998], 66). But "then the analogy is useless" (Joseph Pipa, *Did God Create in Six Days?*, 172). Nor may we suggest that the days are anthropomorphic days, for anthropomorphic language "can be applied to God alone and cannot properly be used of the six days" (Young, *Genesis One*, 58).

To make Genesis 1 a mere literary framework inverts reality: Man's week becomes a pattern for God's! As Young, following G. C. Aalders, remarks: "Man is to 'remember' the Sabbath day, for God has instituted it.... The human week derives validity and significance from the creative week. The fourth commandment constitutes a decisive argument against any non-chronological scheme of the six days of Genesis one" (*Genesis One*, 78-79). If God did not create in six days, we have no reason for Israel's work week—for Israel employed a six-day work week followed by the day of rest *before* Genesis was written.

7. Argument from Plural Expression

Exodus 20:11 and 31:17 also teach that God created the heavens and the earth "in six *days*" (*yammim*). As Robert L. Reymond reminds us: "Ages are never expressed by the word *yammim*" (*Systematic Theology*, 394). In fact, the plural *yammim* occurs 858 times in the Old Testament, and always refers to normal days. Exodus 20:11 (like Gen. 1) lacks any kind of poetic structure; it presents a factual accounting. By this short-hand statement, God sums up His creative activity in a way that not only comports with, but actually *demands* a six-day creative process.

8. Argument from Unusual Expression

Due to the Jewish practice of reckoning days from evening to evening, the temporal pattern "evening and morning" may seem unusual (because it assumes the day *began in the morning*, passes into evening, and closes at the next morning). Cassuto comments: "Whenever clear reference is made to the relationship between a given day and the next, it is precisely sunrise that is accounted the beginning of the second day" (*Genesis*, 1:23). For example, Exodus 12:18 has the fourteenth evening at the conclusion of the fourteenth day (cp. Lev. 23:32). Therefore, Genesis 1 presents literal days reckoned according to the non-ritual pattern—evening closing the daylight time, followed by morning which closes the darkness, thereby *beginning a new day* (e.g., Gen. 19:33-34; Exod. 10:13; 2 Sam. 2:32).

9. Argument from Alternative Idiom

Had Moses intended that six days represent six *eras*, he could have chosen a more fitting expression: *olam*. This word is often translated "forever," but it also means a long period of time (e.g., Exod. 12:24; 21:6; 27:20; 29:28; 30:21). Furthermore, he should not have qualified the days with "evening and morning."

10. Argument from Scholarly Admissions

Remarkably, even liberals and neo-evangelicals who deny six-day creation recognize Moses meant literal days. Herman Gunkel: "The 'days' are of course days and nothing else" (cf. Hasel, "The 'Days' of Creation," 21). Gerhard von Rad: "The seven days are unquestionably to be understood as actual days and as a unique, unrepeatable lapse of time in the world" (*Genesis* 1-11, 65). See also: James Barr (*Fundamentalism*, 40-43); Brown-Driver-Briggs *Lexicon*, 398; Koehler and Baumgartner's *Lexicon*, 372); Holladay's *Lexicon*, 130; and Jenni and Westermann's *Theological Lexicon*, 528. Evangelical Old Testament scholar Victor Hamilton states the matter dogmatically: "Whoever wrote Gen. 1 believed he was talking about literal days" (*Genesis*, 1:54), as does Wenham (*Genesis*, 1:19).

In summary: Moses informs us that God created the whole universe in the span of six chronologically successive periods of twenty-four hours each. Nevertheless, Framework and Day Age advocates see problems.

The Problems for Literal, Chronological Days

1. Objection: "Genesis 2:4 speaks of the entire creation week as a 'day,' showing that 'day' may not be literal."

Response: The phrase here is actually *beyom*, an idiomatic expression meaning "when" (NIV, NRSV, NAB; cp. TDOT 6:15). Besides, even had Genesis 2 used "day" in a different sense, Genesis 1 carefully qualifies its creative days (see points 2 to 5 above).

2. Objection: "Genesis 2:2-3 establishes the seventh day of God's rest, which is ongoing and not a literal day. This shows the preceding six days could be long periods of time."

Response: (1) Contextually, this is an argument from silence—one which contradicts Exodus 20:11. (2) If true, it would imply no fall and curse (Gen. 3), for then God would be continually hallowing and blessing that "ongoing day." In fact, God does *not* bless His *eternal rest*, but a *particular day*. (3) Days 1 to 6 (the actual creation period) are expressly delimited; Day 7 is not. (This is, however, because the creation week has ceased. To mention another "morning" would imply another day followed in that unique period.) Since this is the seventh in a series of six preceding literal days, how can we interpret it other than literally?

3. Objection: "On Day 4, God creates the sun to provide light; but light was created on Day 1. This shows that the days are not chronologically ordered, but thematically cross-linked."

Response: This "problem" is answered in the context. On Day 1 God declares "good" *the newly created light*, but *not* His *separating it from darkness* to form "evening and morning." This is because the *final, providential mechanism* for separating (the sun) is not created until Day 4. Thus, when Day 4 ends, we finally read: "it was good" (Gen. 1:18). This is similar to the separation of the waters above and below on Day 2, which is not declared "good" until the *final* separation from the land on Day 3 (Gen. 1:9). Or like Adam's creation not being "good" (Gen. 2:18) until Eve is separated out of him. Also, Scripture elsewhere suggests light was created separately from the sun (2 Cor. 4:6; Job 38:19-20) and can exist apart from it (Rev. 22:5).

Besides, *most* of the material in Genesis 1 *demands* chronological order —even for Framework advocates. This suggests that the surprising order of light-then-sun is also chronological. Not only is Genesis 1 structured by fifty-five *waw* consecutives [Hebrew, "and"], indicating narrative sequence, but note: Separating the waters on Day 2 requires their prior creation on Day 1 (Gen. 1:2d). Creating the sea on Day 3 must predate the sea creatures of Day 5. Day 3 logically has dry land appearing before land vegetation later that day. Day 3 must predate Day 6, in that land must precede land animals and man. Day 6 must appear as the last stage of creation, in that man forms the obvious climax to God's creation. Day 6 logically has man being created *after* animal life (Days 5 and 6) in that he is commanded to rule over it. Day 7 must conclude the series in that it announces the cessation of creation (Gen. 2:2). And so on.

4. Objection: "The parallelism in the triad of days indicates a *topical* rather than chronological arrangement: Day 1 creates light; Day 4 the light bearers. Day 2's water and sky correspond to Day 5's sea creatures and birds. Day 3's land corresponds to Day 6's land animals and man."

Response: (1) Such parallelism can be *both* literary *and* historical; the two are not mutually exclusive. God can gloriously act according to interesting patterns. For instance, just as the land arises from the water on the third day, so Jesus arises from the tomb on a third day. Likewise, in John 20:15 Mary Magdalene sees Jesus, the Second Adam, in a garden (John 19:41) and assumes He is the gardener. Is this a new Eve encountering the New Adam in a new garden under the new covenant? This theological imagery may very well be true here. But she really did see the resurrected Jesus.

(2) We must not allow the stylistic harmony in the *revelation* of creation to override the emphatic progress in the *history* of creation. The chronological succession leaves too deep an impression upon the narrative to be mere ornamentation.

(3) Numerous discordant features mar the supposed literary framework: For instance, "waters" are created on Day 1 (Gen. 1:2), not Day 2—disrupting the parallel with the water creatures of Day 5. In addition, the creatures of Day 5 are to swim in the "seas" of Day 3. Consequently, the "seas" separated out on Day 3 have no corresponding inhabitant created on its "parallel" day, Day 6. Additional illustrations are pointed out by Young (*Genesis One*, 71-73), Grudem (*Systematic Theology*, 302-03), and others.

5. Objection: "God employed ordinary, slow providence as the prevailing method of creation: Genesis 2:5 demands that the third day had to be *much* longer than twenty-four hours, for the waters removed early on Day 3 leave the land so parched that it desperately needs rain to clothe the landscape with verdure. Yet a full panoply of vegetation appears at the end of that very day, Day 3 (Gen. 1:11)."

Response: This novel, minority interpretation of Genesis 2:5 misses Moses' point. In Genesis 2, Moses is: (a) Setting up Adam's moral test, while (b) *anticipating his failure*.

Note first, the setting: (1) Genesis 2:4 introduces us to what becomes of God's creation (Young, *Genesis One*, 59-61). (2) In describing the whole creative process, Genesis 1 uses only God's name of power (*elohim*); Genesis 2 suddenly introduces His covenant name (*Jehovah God*). (3) Unlike how He creates the animals (en masse by fiat), God creates Adam individually and tenderly (2:7). (4) Genesis 2 focuses on the beautiful garden (2:8-9) and God's gracious provision of a loving helper for Adam (2:18-24). (5) God provides abundant food for Adam (2:16). Thus, the Lord God loves Adam and provides well for him. Would Adam obey Him in such glorious circumstances?

Note second, the anticipation. Opening this new section with the words of Genesis 2:5, the narrative intentionally *anticipates* Adam's fall and God's curse—preparing the reader for the prospect of death (Gen. 2:17): (1) Genesis 2:5 is stating that *before* God cursed the ground with the thorny shrubs (cp. Gen. 3:18a) and before man had to laboriously "cultivate the ground" (cp. Gen. 3:18b-19a), God provided him with all that he needed. (2) The narrative notes God's creation of Adam from the dust (Gen. 2:7), anticipating his rebellion and return thereto (Gen. 3:19b). (3) It tests Adam in terms of his *eating* due to God's abundant provision (Gen. 2:16-17), which foreshadows his *struggling to eat*, due to his failing God's singular prohibition (Gen. 3:17-19a). (4) We learn that at their creation Adam and Eve were "naked and not ashamed" (2:25), anticipating their approaching shame (3:7).

Thus, Genesis 2:5 anticipates *moral failure*, rather than announces *creational method*.

Conclusion

Leading Framework advocate Meredith Kline argues that "as far as the time frame is concerned, with respect to both the duration and sequence of events, the scientist is left free of Biblical constraints in hypothesizing about cosmic origins" ("Space and Time in the Genesis Cosmogony," in *Perspectives on Science and Christian Faith*, 48, 1996, 2). The Scripture clearly teaches that "from the beginning of creation, God made them male and female" (Mark 10:6). But Kline allows billions of years of creating (from the original *ex nihilo* to Adam), teaching that we have only just recently left creation week!

Certainly much more needs to be stated. But I believe the above sufficiently demonstrates the validity of the Westminster Confession, which declares: "It pleased God the Father, Son, and Holy Ghost, for the manifestation of the glory of His eternal power, wisdom, and goodness, in the beginning, to create, or make of nothing, the world, and all things therein whether visible or invisible, in the space of six days; and all very good."

For these reasons I believe in creation "in the space of six days."

CHAPTER SEVEN

God's Law

Theonomy and
The Westminster Confession

Introduction

In 1977, **Greg L. Bahnsen** released a work designed to shed light on a distinctly Biblical view of ethics: *Theonomy in Christian Ethics*.[1] In *Theonomy* an exegetically-based argument was presented for the Christian's "ethical obligation to keep all of God's law" (p. xv) including "the public obligation to promote and enforce obedience to God's law in society as well" (p. xvi). *Theonomy* was "a lengthy, affirmative answer to the question of whether the moral standards (laws) of the Old Testament dispensation were still morally authoritative today, along with New Testament teaching and, if so, whether they provided the Christian with socio-political norms for modern culture."[2] The word "theonomy" simply means "God's Law." Theonomy is the view that God's Old Testament law is still a binding obligation on God's new covenant people, except in those places where the New Testament has rescinded certain features of the law."

Although the theonomic thesis has been attacked from a variety of angles, among Presbyterians its compatibility with confessional theology has become an issue of great debate. Though tertiary to the exegetical and the theological arguments, the historical-confessional defense is important for two reasons:

Historically, Presbyterianism has affirmed a confessionally-based theology. Presbyterian ministers are ordained upon their solemn vow of commitment to that confessional theology.

Ecclesiastically, Presbyterian opponents tend to wield WCF 19:4 against theonomists. For instance, the 1988 Reformed Fellowship's journal *Outlook* cited WCF 19:4 against theonomy as one evidence that "Reformed scholars" have long held that *only* "the moral law, summarized in the Ten Commandments, has been considered binding on the New Testament believer."[3] In a paper presented to the Social Science History Association in 1994 by Reformed Theological Seminary professor J. Ligon Duncan, theonomy is accused of "ignoring the context of 19:4..., abstracting the meaning of 'general equity' from its historic legal and theological context, and failing to appreciate the Biblical, theological genius of the Assembly's categorization."[4]

I will present a three-fold historical argument for the Confessional compatibility of theonomic ethics based on (1) theonomic admissions by our opponents; (2) theonomic specimens from the divines; and (3) theonomic explanations of our Confession.

I. Theonomic Admissions by Our Opponents

As it so happens, theonomy's confessional compatibility is so strong that some of the most noteworthy theonomic opponents from the reformed community will even grant the confessional argument and move to other considerations. Note the following few samples.

Meredith G. Kline

Surely one of the most vehement and best-known reformed opponents of theonomy is Old Testament scholar Meredith G. Kline, who calls theonomy the "Chalcedon aberration" (based on the influence of R. J. Rushdoony's Chalcedon Foundation). In his remarkably vehement attack, Kline admits that theonomy is the "old-new error," that is, an error "new" to our time though found in the "old" Confession itself:

> At the same time it must be said that Chalcedon is not without roots in respectable ecclesiastical tradition. It is in fact a revival of certain teachings contained in the Westminster Confession of Faith—at least in the Confession's original formulations. These

particular elements in the Confession, long since rejected as manifestly unbiblical by the mass of those who stand in that confessional tradition (as well as by virtually all other students of the Scriptures), have been subjected to official revision. The revision, however, has left us with standards whose proper legal interpretation is perplexed by ambiguities, and the claim of Chalcedon is that it is the true champion of confessional orthodoxy. Ecclesiastical courts operating under the Westminster Confession of Faith are going to have their problems, therefore, if they should be of a mind to bring the Chalcedon aberration under their judicial scrutiny.[5]

In this article, Kline even calls for a revision of the Confession of Faith to root out these theonomic elements. Ironically, were Kline's call for a revision followed, the remarkable result would be to exclude the original framers of the Confession from Presbyterian churches!

R. Laird Harris

Another respected opponent of theonomy is the noted Old Testament scholar from the Presbyterian Church in America, R. Laird Harris. Although he does not offer as much on the confessional question, he clearly works from the same assumption as Kline:

Theonomy was until recently a little-used word. It is Greek for God's law. Etymologically it refers to an idea which all Christians have always accepted—that the law of God is a wonderful revelation of Himself and of His will to His Church and is to be prized by us all and obeyed. But the word is now being used to designate a new idea gaining ground in some circles, particularly those emphasizing Reformed doctrine, that the governments of the world today should be guided in their judicial decisions by all the legislation of the Old Testament and, in particular, should assess the Old Testament penalties for an infraction of those laws, where civil or religious. Dr. Bahnsen's book, *Theonomy in Christian Ethics*, is an extended explanation of and defense of this theory. Due to the radical nature of the theory, its important consequences, and significant following, the view deserves extensive treatment.

The view is not really new; it is just new in our time. It was the usual view through the Middle Ages, was not thrown over by the

Reformers and was espoused by the Scottish Covenanters who asked the Long Parliament to make Presbyterianism the religion of the three realms—England, Scotland, and Ireland.[6]

Sinclair Ferguson

In the important full-length reformed critique of theonomy, Sinclair Ferguson of Westminster Theological Seminary engages the confessional question in his chapter titled: "An Assembly of Theonomists?" Interestingly, he admits the influence of theonomy on the Confession: "Essentially, Bahnsen accepts the doctrinal orthodoxy of the original text [of the Confession]. Whether or not this is in conflict with the intention of the American Presbyterian emendation of the Confession, it is certainly in keeping with the traditional Scottish Reformed understanding of it."[7] Indeed, he asserts:

> It should be noted that in many instances the practical implications of theonomy may not necessarily be a denial of the teaching of the Westminster Confession. The words of Chapter XIX, IV can be understood to include the view that the Mosaic penalties may be applied by the Christian magistrate (if "general equity" so dictates). We have already noted that such views were widespread among the Divines in relation to specific crimes. But this is simply to recognize that there may be common ground *in practice* between the Confession's teaching and theonomy.[8]

D. Clair Davis

Continuing from the same book for which Ferguson writes (and in a similarly and refreshingly mild manner), Clair Davis, Professor of Church History at Westminster Theological Seminary, notes: "It is easy to argue that the Westminster Confession's commitment to the general equity of Old Testament law provides ample justification for theonomic clarification of that equity."[9]

II. Theonomic Specimens from the Divines

We discover the reason for such admissions in the writings of the Westminster Divines themselves. Interestingly, while denying the presence of the theonomic *theory* in the Confession, Ferguson admits the theonomic *practice*:

- Such views were widespread among the Divines in relation to specific crimes. But this is simply to recognize that there may be common ground *in practice* between the Confession's teaching and theonomy.[10]

- The strongest position a theonomist could adopt *on the basis of the* Confession would be that it did not *a priori* reject the application of the Mosaic judicial punishment for crimes considered *seriatim*. But *theoretical* theonomy as such is not the teaching of the Westminster Confession of Faith.[11]

- It is essential to notice that there may be similarities in the practical outworking of these two principles. . . . But whatever similarities may arise because of the Confession's qualifying clause, it would be absurd to suggest that the principles themselves are identical.[12]

With these types of admissions, the theonomist is practically handed the Confession as a defensive historical instrument for *applied theonomy*—despite charges that *methodological theonomy* is lacking among the divines. The evidence is abundantly clear in the writings of many of the Westminster divines, as the following citations will prove.

As I begin this survey of material, the reader should bear two notes in mind: (1) Where necessary, I have updated the seventeenth century style to make it more readable. For example, "He must not punish no sinnes" becomes "He must not punish sins." (2) Some of the citations will assert positions that even theonomists do not maintain, but which arise from a theonomic-like approach to civil ethics. Consequently, as I cite the Westminster divines on certain issues, I will show their theonomic tendencies, even where those tendencies go beyond modern theonomy. I do not endorse all of the views cited.

George Gillespie (1613-1648)

One of the leading Westminster divines was Scottish commissioner George Gillespie. He not only voted for the Westminster Confession of Faith, he helped write it. Hetherington claims that Gillespie "became one of the most prominent members of that August assembly, although the youngest man and minister of the whole."[13] In fact, "he took an equally active and influential part in the framing of the Confession of

Faith and the Catechisms, which embodied the doctrinal decisions of the Assembly."[14]

In *Wholesome Severity Reconciled with Christian Liberty* Gillespie offers remarkably theonomic observations:

> (2) Christ's words (Matt. 5:17, KJV), "Think not that I am come to destroy the Law or the Prophets, I am not come to destroy, but to fulfill," are comprehensive of the judicial law, it being a part of the law of Moses. Now he could not fulfill the judicial law, except either by his practice, or by teaching others still to observe it; not by his own practice, for he would not condemn the adulteress (John 8:11), nor divide the inheritance (Luke 12:13-14). Therefore, it must be by His doctrine for our observing it.
>
> (3) If Christ in His sermon (Matt. 5) would teach that the moral law belongs to us Christians, in so much as He vindicates it from the false glosses of the scribes and Pharisees, then He meant to hold forth the judicial law concerning moral trespasses as belonging unto us also; for He vindicates and interprets the judicial law, as well as the moral (Matt. 5:38), an eye for an eye, etc.
>
> (4) If God would have the moral law transmitted from the Jewish people to the Christian people; then He would also have the judicial laws transmitted from the Jewish Magistrate to the Christian Magistrate: there being the same reason of immutability in the punishments, which is in the offenses.[15]

Samuel Rutherford (1600-1661)

Another of the Scottish divines, Samuel Rutherford, was a theologian of great stature and influence. Hetherington notes of him that: "While he attended that Assembly, he greatly distinguished himself by his skill in debate, his eloquence in preaching, and his great learning and ability as an author. Few works of that age surpass, or even equal, those which were produced by Rutherford during that intensely laborious period of his life."[16]

Rutherford writes of the civil magistrate in his most important work *Lex, Rex*:

> The execution of their office is an act of the just Lord of heaven and earth, not only by permission, but according to God's revealed will in His word; their judgment is not the judgment of

men, but of the LORD (2 Chron. 19:6), and their throne is the throne of God (1 Chron. 22:10). Jerome saith, to punish murderers and sacrilegious persons is not bloodshed, but the ministry and service of good laws. So, if the king be a living law by office, and the law put in execution which God hath commanded, then, as the moral law is by divine institution, so must the officer of God be, who is *custos et vindex legis divnae*, the keeper, preserver, and avengers of God's law.[17]

Later he observes in a similar vein (44:16): "As the king is under God's law both in commanding and in exacting active obedience, so is he under the same regulating law of God, in punishing or demanding of us passive subjection, and as he may not command what he will, but what the King of kings warranteth him to command, so may he not punish as he will, but by warrant also of the Supreme Judge of all the earth."[18]

In another work entitled *The Due Right of Presbyteries, or, a Peaceable Plea*, Rutherford writes:

It is clear the question must be thus stated, for all the laws of the Old Testament (which we hold in their Moral equity to be perpetual) that are touching blasphemies, heresies, solicitation to worship false Gods and the breach of which the Godly Magistrate was to punish, command or forbid only such things as may be proved by two or three witnesses, and which *husband and wife are not to conceal,* and from which all *Israel* must abstain for fear of the like punishment. Deut. 13:8, 9, 10, 11; Deut. 17:5, 6; Lev. 20:1, 2, 3, 4. But opinions in the mind, acts of the understanding, can never be proved by witnesses and such as neither *Magistrates* nor *Church* can censure.[19]

Other Divines

Jeremiah Burroughs (1599–1646), speaking of a capital-sanctions text considered an embarrassment to theonomy,[20] commented on Deuteronomy 13:

Let not any put off this Scripture, saying, This is in the Old Testament but we find no such thing in the gospel, for we find the same thing almost the same words used in a prophecy of the times of the gospel (Zech. 13:3). [Of Zech. 13 he observed:] You must understand this by that in Deuteronomy. The meaning is not that his father or mother should presently run a knife into him, but that though they begat him, yet they should be the means to bring him to condign punishment, even the taking away of his life; those who were the instruments of his life, should now be the instruments of his death.[21]

Herbert Palmer (1601-1647), argued from a theonomic methodology, that "this general rule gives me leave to assert and commend to your most serious considerations and consciences: That whatsoever Law of God, or command of His, we find recorded in the Law-book, in either of the volumes of God's statute, the New Testament or the Old Testament, remains obligatory to us, unless we can prove it to be expired, or repealed. So it is with the statute-law of this nation, or of any nation."[22]

William Reyner (d. 1666), referring to the capital sanctions against idolatry, argued: "This duty is principally incumbent upon the magistrate, who is to execute judgment of the Lord, not arbitrarily as he himself pleaseth; but according to the rule of the Word, both for matter and manner."[23]

Richard Vines (1600-1655) vigorously argued for the continuance of capital sanctions against blasphemers:

> For the blasphemous and seditious heretics, both Lutherans and others of the Reformed churches do agree that they may be punished capitally, that is for their blasphemy or sedition. But the Socinian stands out here also, and denies it, alleging that the punishment of false prophets in that was *especiali jure* by special law granted to the *Israelites*, and therefore you must not look (saith the Socinian) into the Old Testament for a rule of proceeding against false prophets and blasphemers: Nor (saith *Calvin* and *Catharinus*) can you find in the New Testament any precept for the punishment of thieves, traitors, adulterers, witches, murders and the like, and yet they may, or at least some of them may be capitally punished: for the gospel destroys not the just laws of civil policy or commonwealths.[24]

Along with these citations from commissioners to the Westminster Assembly, it would be easy to cite page after page of equally compelling references from the writings of like-minded Puritans of the era. Indeed, Foulner's *Theonomy and the Westminster Confession* does just that—oftentimes with helpful interpretive footnotes responding to theonomic critics.[25]

III. Theonomic Explanations of our Confession

We must now turn our attention to the swirling vortex of the debate: the Confession's statement in 19:4:

> IV. To them also, as a body politic, He gave sundry judicial laws, which expired together with the State of that people; not obliging any other now, further than the general equity thereof may require.

Certainly a cursory reading of 19:4 sounds contra-theonomic. Does it not declare the judicial laws "expired"? Are we not informed that they are "not obliging any other now"? Does it not reduce the concrete judicial laws to a vague "general equity"? This certainly appears anti-theonomic. But first looks are often deceiving.

Historical Presumption

Just as we must understand the *occasional* nature of the New Testament epistles if we are to more properly understand and more deeply appreciate them,[26] so must we understand the historical setting of the Westminster Assembly if we are to grasp the reasoning of the divines. We are all children of our times; we all speak from our historical contexts. And so it is with the Westminster Standards: they were not alien intrusions into a placid life of political indifference. In fact, the calling of the Assembly itself was fraught with political significance and urged on the basis of political pressures.

The Early Reformers

First, the theonomic inclination was clearly established among the early Reformers. Calvin's Geneva—though neither perfect nor wholly consistent—rightly serves as an experimental model of theonomic political theory in practice.[27] Calvin had strong predilections toward the application of God's Law to contemporary socio-political matters—his much abused statement at 4:20:14 in his *Institutes* notwithstanding.[28]

In his commentary on the much maligned thirteenth chapter of

Deuteronomy, **John Calvin** (1509-1564) noted: "Whoever shall now contend that it is unjust to put heretics and blasphemers to death will knowingly and willingly incur their very guilt. This is not laid down on human authority; it is God who speaks and prescribes a perpetual rule for His Church." He even scathingly criticizes those who would oppose his position: "Some scoundrel or other gainsays this, and sets himself against the author of life and death. What insolence is this. . . . God has once pronounced what is His will, for we must needs abide by His inviolable decree."[29] As Philip Schaff notes: "Calvin's plea for the right and duty of the Christian magistrate to punish heresy by death, stands or falls with his theocratic theory and the binding authority of the Mosaic code. His arguments are chiefly drawn from the Jewish laws against idolatry and blasphemy, and from the examples of the pious kings of Israel."[30] (For a contemporary theonomic understanding of the heresy laws, see my "Church Sanctions in the Epistle to the Hebrews."[31])

Martin Bucer (1491-1551), a great influence on Calvin, argued:

> But since no one can describe an approach more equitable and wholesome to the commonwealth than that which God describes in His law, it is certainly the duty of all kings and princes who recognize that God has put them over His people that they follow most studiously His own method of punishing evildoers.[32]

Bucer immediately annexes to this statement a list of capital crimes from the Mosaic legislation, and then notes a little later that the king must "for every single crime" impose "those penalties which the Lord Himself has sanctioned."[33]

John Knox (1514-1572) commented on Deuteronomy 17 as follows (please note again: the modern theonomist does *not* follow his exposition; nevertheless his presumption of the authoritative and binding applicability of God's Law is clear):

> If any thinks that the fore written law did bind the Jews only, let the same man consider that the election of a king and appointing of judges did neither appertain to the ceremonial law, neither yet was it merely judicial; but that it did flow from the moral law, as an ordinance having respect to the conservation of both the tables.... [Consequently] it is evident, that the office of the king

or supreme magistrate, has respect to the moral law, and to the conservation of both tables.[34]

Swiss Reformer and successor to Ulrich Zwingli, **Johann Heinrich Bullinger** (1504-1575) wrote that "the substance of God's judicial laws is not taken away or abolished, but the ordering and imitation of them is placed in the arbitrament of good Christian princes."[35] In chapter 30 on the Civil Magistrate, Bullinger wrote of the civil ruler:

> Let him govern the people, committed to him of God, with good laws, made according to the Word of God in his hands, and look that nothing be taught contrary thereunto. . . . Therefore let him draw forth this sword of God against all malefactors, seditious persons, thieves, murderers, oppressors, blasphemers, perjured persons, and all those whom God has commanded him to punish or even to execute.

Thus, we discover in these influential Reformers a clear pattern of theonomically-inclined socio-political theory. These are deep tributaries feeding the Puritan stream of thought.

Westminster Contemporaries

Second, the contemporary Reformed influence beyond the Westminster Assembly clearly adopted a theonomic-like conviction regarding the binding obligation of God's judicial laws in the civil sphere. Here I have space only for a few samples from the wider Puritan community.

Prominent Massachusetts Bay pastor **John Cotton** (1584-1652) published an influential work which became the foundation of the civil code of Massachusetts: *An Abstract of the Laws of New England, as They are Now Established*. This work and the civil code based upon it quote extensively from the Mosaic code (Greg Bahnsen included this document as Appendix 3 in *Theonomy in Christian Ethics*, Covenant Media Foundation, 1977, 2005).

Another Massachusetts Puritan, **Thomas Shepard** (1605-1649) argued that "the judicial laws, some of them being hedges and fences to safeguard both moral and ceremonial precepts, their binding power was therefore mixed and various, for those which did safeguard any moral law, (which is perpetual,) whether by just punishments or otherwise, do still morally bind all nations." He continued by noting: "God would have all nations preserve their fences forever, as He would have that law preserved forever which these safeguard."[36]

James Durham (1622-1658) distinguished between the three categories of law and noted that "the judicial law is for regulating outward society, and for government, and doth generally (excepting what was peculiar to the people of Israel) agree with the moral law."[37] Durham classed the capital sanction for adultery in the "moral" category when he observed that adultery "is a heinous crime worthy to be punished by the judge. The laws of man should take order with such a sin, and the moral law of God taught that such a sin deserved death (Deut. 22:22), not only in the woman, as some would have it only, but also in the man."[38]

The Records of the New Haven Colony (1641-1644), *Connecticut Archives*, presented the following theonomic statement:

> The judicial law of God given by Moses and expounded in other parts of scripture, so far as it is a hedge and a fence to the moral laws, and neither ceremonial nor typical nor had any reference to Canaan, hath an everlasting *equity* it, and should be the rule of our proceedings.... It was ordered that the judicial laws of God, as they were delivered by Moses...be a rule to all the courts in this jurisdiction in their proceedings against offenders.

Third, as I show above under "Theonomic Specimens," the Westminster divines themselves display a marked propensity to theonomic political ethics. In fact, two of the leading divines, George Gillespie and Samuel Rutherford, may be positively designated theonomists. And, based on their statements, surely none of them would *oppose* theonomy.

After all this historical research is sorted and analyzed, how can the Westminster Standards be opposed to a theonomic-like employment of the judicial laws? Was not their Reformational history conducive to theonomic reflection? Did not their framers frequently apply Mosaic penalties in a judicial context? Did they not vigorously argue for the continuing validity of the Mosaic sanctions? If we may not positively assert that Westminster was "an assembly of theonomists" (to employ Ferguson's phrase), are we left to scratch our heads and wonder if this was an assembly of schizophrenics?

Philosophical Complexion

In light of all the historical and literary evidence for the Puritans' application of the Mosaic judicials to contemporary political matters, we should not be surprised that the Standards share this same family complexion. This is true even in the 1788 Americanized edition of the Confession (as Kline laments), but is especially obvious in the original documents adopted by the Westminster Assembly. I will summarize the theonomic tendencies of confessional political philosophy under two heads.

Westminster and the Civil Magistrate

First, the Confession's chapter on the civil magistrate clearly establishes a theonomically inclined political philosophy. This is most clearly delineated in WCF 23; section 1 reads:

> God, the supreme Lord and King of all the world, has ordained civil magistrates, to be, under Him, over the people, for His own glory, and the public good: and, to this end, has armed them with the power of the sword, for the defence and encouragement of them that are good, and for the punishment of evil doers.

The Westminster socio-political philosophy asserts that:

1. God positively ordains civil authority. We see the theonomic tendency initially in the Confession's non-neutralist affirmation that "God, the supreme Lord and King of all the world, has ordained civil magistrates" (23:1a). Here we have—quite in keeping with the full-orbed Calvinistic theology of the Confession elsewhere, although not all that controversial—the declaration that the civil magistracy is positively established by God. Civil rule is not merely an evolutionary sociological happenstance; nor is it an aspect of man's ethical rebellion against God; nor is it a matter of indifference to God. The Lord positively ordains civil rule over men gathered in societies, so that to resist civil authority in its "lawful power, or the lawful exercise of it" is to "resist the ordinance of God" (WCF 20:4).

In fact, here we learn that the civil magistrate may "lawfully" punish men for:

> publishing of such opinions, or maintaining of such practices, as are contrary to the light of nature, or to the *known principles*

of Christianity (whether concerning faith, worship, or conversation), or to the power of godliness; or, such erroneous opinions or practices, as either in their own nature, or in the manner of publishing or maintaining them, are destructive to the external peace and order which Christ has established in the Church, they may lawfully be called to account, and proceeded against, by the censures of the Church *and by the power of the civil magistrate* (20:4b).[39]

2. God sovereignly limits (i.e., morally constrains) civil authority. In addition to the previous observation which is rather widely accepted, we find a phrase more narrowly conceived: the magistrate is "to be under Him" (23:1a). "God, the supreme Lord and King of all the world, has ordained civil magistrates, to be, under Him."

Here the Confession rebukes the then current notion of the divine right of kings: even the king is *under* God. Consequently, he is deemed a servant of God and morally bound to recognize his own servant position in the world, that is, *under God* though *over the people*. Larger Catechism (LC) 124 designates magistrates as "superiors" ordained by God to be obeyed: "By father and mother, in the fifth commandment, are meant, not only natural parents, but *all superiors* in age and gifts; and *especially such as, by God's ordinance, are over us in place of authority*, whether in family, church, or *commonwealth*."

The civil magistrate is a "superior" who must govern *lawfully*, that is, according to God's Law. Thus, LC 127 reads:

> The honor which inferiors owe to their superiors is, all due reverence in heart, word, and behavior; prayer and thanksgiving for them; imitation of their virtues and graces; willing obedience to their *lawful commands* and counsels; due submission to their corrections; fidelity to, defense and maintenance of their persons and authority, according to their several ranks, and the nature of their places; bearing with their infirmities, and covering them in love, that so they may be an honor to them and to their government.

One Confessional illustration of "lawful" civil authority is the keeping and promoting of the sabbath, which is obviously an element in God's Law:

The charge of keeping the sabbath is more specially directed to governors of families, and *other superiors,* because they are bound not only to keep it themselves, *but to see that it be observed by all those that are under their charge;* and because they are prone ofttimes to hinder them by employments of their own" (LC 118).

Another illustration is the Confession's disallowing incestuous relations *as defined in God's Law:*

Nor can such incestuous marriages ever be made lawful by any law of man or consent of parties, so as those persons may live together as man and wife. [The man may not marry any of his wife's kindred, nearer in blood than he may of his own: nor the woman of her husband's kindred, nearer in blood than of her own]" (WCF 24:1; cp. LC 139).[40]

The word "lawful" in the context of the Standards refers to those things *allowed by express revelation in God's Word.*

Westminster Proof-texts

Second, the Westminster Standards freely cite from Old Testament judicial laws to justify their creedal stance. If those laws were wholly abrogated, their employment would be futile.[41]

In WCF 20:4, the divines warn of speaking against the "known principles of Christianity"; such would subject one to the threat of punishment by "the civil magistrate." The justification for such, as we see often from their other writings, is the infamous capital sanction against idolatry, Deuteronomy 13. Not only is this judicial law their first proof-text, but they employ others enforcing the Sabbath (Neh. 13:15-25) and paralleling the Deuteronomy passage (Zech. 13:2-3).

In WCF 22:3, oaths and vows are governed by Numbers 5:12, 19, 21. Civil suppression of "blasphemies and heresies" in WCF 23:3 is proven by referring to capital sanctions in Leviticus 24:16 and Deuteronomy 13:5. Laws forbidding Biblically-defined consanguinity are cited in WCF 24:4: Leviticus 18 and 20:19-21. Divorce legislation in WCF 26 is justified by Deuteronomy 24:1-4. False religion must be removed by the civil magistrate, for God requires such in Deuteronomy 7:5 (LC 108) and Deuteronomy 13:6-12 (LC 109). Capital punishment is morally justified in LC 136 by citing Numbers 35:16-21,31 and Exodus 21:18-36. The capital sanction against bestiality is appended to LC 139: Leviticus 20:15-16. Restitution is required for theft in LC 141, as required by Leviticus 6:2-5.

Interestingly, Deuteronomy 13 is cited several times in the Standards: WCF 20:4; 23:3; LC 109; and LC 145. In addition, a perusal of Stephen Pribble's extremely helpful *Scripture Index to the Westminster Standards* provides evidence of scores of references to the Mosaic judicial legislation.[42]

Lexical Implications

Now let us consider WCF 19:4 specifically. What are we to make of the Confession's express statements regarding the judicial laws? What do the divines mean when they state: "To them [the Jews] also, as a body politic, He gave sundry judicial laws, which expired together with the State of that people; not obliging any other now, further than the general equity thereof may require" (19:4)?

Ceremonial Abrogation

First, we should note that the divines treat the judicial laws in a fundamentally different way than the ceremonial laws. This observation, though not conclusive, will put us on the right track for arriving at their intent.

When we compare the statement in 19:3 on the ceremonial law with 19:4 on the judicial law, we discover a much stronger word used in removing our obligation to the ceremonial: "*All* which ceremonial laws are now *abrogated*, under the New Testament." According to the *Oxford English Dictionary*, the word "abrogated" means "abolished by authority, annulled." Indeed, the word "abrogate" is derived from Latin legal language, being a compound of *ab* ("away") and *rogare* ("to propose a law"). Thus, the Confession states that "all" of these ceremonial laws are positively "abrogated," as by decree, i.e., the revelation of "the New Testament." The statement on the judicial law, to which I will return shortly, is milder: "He gave sundry judicial laws, which *expired*." Neither is it attached to the arrival of the "New Testament."

In WCF 7:5, we read of the nature of the Old Testament economy which is now defunct:

> This covenant was differently administered in the time of the law, and in the time of the Gospel: under the law it was administered by promises, prophecies, sacrifices, circumcision, the paschal lamb, and other types and ordinances delivered to the people of the Jews, all foresignifying Christ to come; which were, for that time, sufficient and efficacious, through the operation of the Spirit, to instruct and build up the elect in faith in the promised Messiah, by whom they had full remission of sins, and eternal salvation; and is called the Old Testament.

The Old Testament economy was "differently administered in the time of the law." But the positive difference of that administration—which characterizes the oldness of the Old Testament—is defined in terms of *ceremonies* "all foresignifying Christ to come" which refer to the "full remission of sins, and eternal salvation." The Old Testament economy, then, is different, not in regard to its moral character or judicial makeup, but rather in its "types . . . foresignifying Christ." Nothing is said of the judicial law as an aspect of the difference in the new administration. As 19:3 says: the ceremonial law is "abrogated under the New Testament," which is precisely—and *only*—what we see here in chapter 7.

When the New Testament, which "abrogates" the Old Testament, finally arrives, its difference lies in its conclusive character, as opposed to the typical character of the Old. WCF 7:6 reads:

> Under the Gospel, when Christ, the substance, was exhibited, the ordinances in which this covenant is dispensed are the preaching of the Word, and the administration of the sacraments of Baptism and the Lord's Supper: which, though fewer in number, and administered with more simplicity, and less outward glory, yet, in them, it is held forth in more fullness, evidence, and spiritual efficacy, to all nations, both Jews and Gentiles; and is called the New Testament. There are not therefore two covenants of grace, differing in substance, but one and the same, under various dispensations.

Here the Confession once again fails to describe the covenantal difference of the New Testament by reference to judicial stipulations or civil ethics. In fact, this anti-ceremonial theme, along with a silence regarding judicial matters, continues in WCF 20. There in section 1 we read that "under the New Testament, the liberty of Christians is further enlarged, *in their freedom from the yoke of the ceremonial law,* to which the Jewish Church was subjected." Again: the focal difference is on the *ceremonial,* not the judicial law. Our liberty does not involve a liberty from the judicial law, but from the ceremonial. All of this will become more evident below.

Judicial Expiration

Second, in 19:4 the milder term "expired" implies inherent elements in the judicial laws that simply fail to function any longer. They are not positively "abrogated"; they are not judicially repealed. If the same result befalls both the judicial and the ceremonial laws, as the anti-theonomic position avers, why were the judicial laws not declared "abrogated," then reference made to the New Testament for judicial principles? The Confession, after all, has a clear concern for political and judicial ethics. And why do the judicial laws appear frequently in the proof-texts for the Larger Catechism exposition of the Ten Commandments? These are inexplicable on the anti-theonomic position.

Admittedly, the Confession does note that the judicial laws "expired." That is, they expired along with the Jewish "State," the "body politic." A hermeneutically sound exegesis of WCF 19:4 must recognize that the expiring of the judicial laws *in the context* refers to their association with the particular "State" of Israel: the laws as *literally expressed* were given to a specific, historically defined "body politic." The very nature of case law is to provide *sample,* concrete illustrations of legally chargeable offenses for a particular culture and time. Case laws do not enumerate each and every conceivable criminal infraction. Consequently, were the Mosaic judicial laws to continue in toto, then we would be morally obligated to build fences around our roofs, use stoning as the method of capital punishment, provide three cities of refuge, punish certain ceremonial infractions, and so forth. Neither the Puritans, nor the Confession, nor modern theonomists argue for such. The Israel-related, time-bound literal expression of the case laws "expired," because the specific "State" within which they derived their sense expired.

That this statement in the Confession is not functionally equivalent to a wholesale abrogation, as in the case of the ceremonial laws, is evident in the divines' choice of a conceptually different term: "expired," rather than "abrogated." We also see a difference in the proviso added: "not obliging any other now, further than the general equity thereof may require." Clearly, the "general equity" continues from the judicial law, though no such equity continues from the ceremonial law. In fact, one of the proof-texts for this section on the continuing general equity is Matthew 5:17, *the* theonomic proof-text: "Do not think that I came to abolish the Law or the Prophets; I did not come to abolish, but to fulfill." Obviously the divines did not equate "expired" with "abolish" (Matt. 5:17) or "abrogated" (WCF 19:3).

Elsewhere we read in WCF 6:6 that "*every* sin, both original and actual, being a transgression of the righteous law of God, and contrary thereunto, does in its own nature, bring guilt upon the sinner, whereby he is bound over to the wrath of God, and curse of the law, and so made subject to death, with *all* miseries spiritual, *temporal*, and eternal." In 19:6 we read: "the threatenings of [the law] serve to show what even their *sins deserve*; and *what afflictions, in this life, they may expect* for them, although freed from the curse thereof threatened in the law." Consequently, the Confession fences in and defends the moral law by allowing the continuance of "*all* . . . temporal" consequences of breaching it. That these "temporal" consequences include temporal sanctions imposed by the civil magistrate is obvious in that "God, the supreme Lord and King of all the world, has ordained civil magistrates, to be, under Him" and "for the punishment of evil doers" (WCF 23:1).

Thus, the divines allow revealed, temporal, judicial responses to guide the magistrate in the New Testament era. The Confession clearly declares this in the original version of WCF 23:3, where we read of one of the civil magistrates' duty that "all blasphemies and heresies be suppressed." Here the divines cited Leviticus 24:16 and Deuteronomy 13:5 as proof-texts. Obviously, an "expired" law still "requiring" a "general equity" is fundamentally different from an "abrogated" law (as per the ceremonial laws).

Furthermore, in LC 108 we read the obligation that devolves upon men "according to each one's place and calling":

The duties required in the second commandment are, the receiving, observing, and keeping pure and entire, all such religious worship and ordinances as God has instituted in His Word; particularly prayer and thanksgiving in the name of Christ; the reading, preaching, and hearing of the Word; the administration and receiving of the sacraments; church government and discipline; the ministry and maintenance thereof; religious fasting; swearing by the name of God, and vowing unto Him: as also the disapproving, detesting, opposing, all false worship; and, *according to each one's place and calling, removing it, and all monuments of idolatry.*

The confessional view of "calling" includes the civil magistrate in his public duty: "It is lawful for Christians to accept and execute the office of a magistrate, when *called* thereunto" (WCF 23:2). Thus, of the second commandment, Larger Catechism 108 directs the civil ruler to oppose and remove all monuments of idolatry—*as required in various judicial laws of the Old Testament.* The proof-texts cited include Deuteronomy 7:5, a judicial case law. The next question, a follow-up to LC 108, also cites Deuteronomy 13:6-8.

Larger Catechism 99, speaking on the fundamental moral law contained in the Ten Commandments, agrees:

That what is forbidden or commanded to ourselves, we are bound, *according to our places,* to endeavor that it may be avoided or performed by others, *according to the duty of their places.* That in what is commanded to others, we are bound, *according to our places and callings,* to be helpful to them; and to take heed of partaking with others in what is forbidden them.

As noted previously, the unedited original of WCF 23:3 says of the magistrate that "he has *authority,* and it is his *duty,* to take order that unity and peace be preserved in the Church, that the truth of God be kept pure and entire, that *all blasphemies and heresies be suppressed.*" Here again we find reference to Deuteronomy 13 in the proof-texts. Though the modern theonomic expression might not urge precisely this response to heresy, who can assert that the Confession has wholly removed the judicial laws from consideration? Perhaps the Confession is *more* theonomic than modern theonomists! But it is certainly not *less* so.

Equity Continuation

Third, the exclusionary clause in 19:4 reminds us that though the judicial laws have "expired," their "general equity" has not. Indeed, their equity will "require" (not: "suggest" or "encourage" or "allow") application: "To them also, as a body politic, He gave sundry judicial laws, which expired together with the State of that people; not obliging any other now, further than the *general equity* thereof may *require*." Here we must determine the meaning of the phrase "general equity" in its historical and Confessional context.

According to the Oxford English Dictionary, the term "equity," when applied to matters of legal jurisprudence, speaks of the "recourse to general principles of justice . . . to correct or supplement the provisions of the law." The "equity of a statute," therefore, involves "the construction of a statute according to its reason and spirit, so as to make it apply to cases for which it does not expressly provide." Obviously the divines would not assert that we need "to correct" God's Law, for it is His very word (WCF 1:4). Consequently, the remaining "equity" must speak of the underlying principles, the "reason and spirit" of the Law when we "make it apply to cases for which it does not expressly provide." The Law's equity, then, extends to modern situations (it is still binding; it is "required"), even though the particular ancient and ceremonially-dominated features of Israel no longer exist (it "expired" because given to a specific "body politic").

Perhaps one of the best tools for understanding the Confession at this point is Scripture itself—particularly the King James Version. The Assembly wrote the Confession of Faith in Elizabethan English identical with the KJV, even employing its phraseology and using it as the text for the Scripture proof-texts. As Donald Remillard notes in his *A Contemporary Edition of the Westminster Confession of Faith:* "The initial text of the Westminster Confession of Faith was presented to the English speaking people in 1646. This occurred only thirty-five years after the publication of the King James version of the Bible in 1611. Consequently, its original grammar and vocabulary reflect a mode of communication long dated and 'foreign' to contemporary forms and styles of English usage."[43] We may reasonably conclude that the term "equity" in WCF

19:4 would have the same linguistic function as that in the KJV, which the Confession reflects.

The word "equity" appears numerous times in the KJV, several of which show that God's Law is the standard of equitable righteousness and of sure justice. Psalm 98:9b reads: "with righteousness shall He judge the world, and the people with *equity*." Notice the parallel of "righteousness" and "equity." God's Law is inherently and necessarily righteous, as Deuteronomy 4:8 (NASB) informs us: "What great nation is there that has statutes and judgments as righteous as this whole law which I am setting before you today?" Following the Mosaic pattern here in Deuteronomy 4, God's righteousness is frequently paralleled with God's Law in Scripture (Isa. 42:21; 51:7; Hab. 1:4; Rom. 3:21; 7:12). In fact, Psalm 119 *frequently* parallels God's law, statutes, ordinances with "righteousness" (Ps. 119:7, 40, 62, 75, 106, 121, 123, 137-138, 142, 144, 160, 164, 172).

Psalm 99:4 (KJV) states that "the king's strength also loveth judgment; thou dost establish *equity*, thou executest judgment and righteousness in Jacob." Notice the parallel of *equity* with the king's judgment and righteousness. Proverbs 1:3 (KJV) urges us "to receive the instruction of wisdom, justice, and judgment, and *equity*." Notice the inclusion of *equity* with wisdom, justice, and judgment. Proverbs 2:9 (KJV) follows suit when it observes: "Then shalt thou understand righteousness, and judgment, and *equity*; yea, every good path."

Isaiah 11:4a (KJV) prophesies that "with righteousness shall He judge the poor, and reprove with *equity* for the meek of the earth." Isaiah 59:14 (KJV) laments that "judgment is turned away backward, and justice standeth afar off: for truth is fallen in the street, and *equity* cannot enter." Micah 3:9 rebukes Israel: "Hear this, I pray you, ye heads of the house of Jacob, and princes of the house of Israel, that abhor judgment, and pervert all *equity*."

This concept of the continuing, obligatory equity of God's Law was common among the Puritans in the era of the Westminster Assembly. According to historian Thomas Hutchinson, Thomas Cartwright "who had a chief hand in reducing puritanism to a system, held, that the magistrate was bound to adhere to the judicial law of Moses, and might not punish or pardon otherwise than they prescribed."[44] Yet in 1575

Cartwright observed, in keeping with both the theonomic principle and the Confessional equity-approach to law, observed:

> And, as for the judicial law, forasmuch as there are some of them made in regard of the region where they were given, and of the people to whom they were given, the prince and magistrate, keeping the substance and *equity* of them (as it were the marrow), may change the circumstance of them, as the times and places and manners of the people shall require. But to say that any magistrate can save the life of blasphemers, contemptuous and stubborn idolaters, murderers, adulterers, incestuous persons, and such like, which God by His judicial law hath commanded to be put to death, I do utterly deny, and am ready to prove, if that pertained to this question.[45]

Puritan William Perkins concurred with Cartwright's approach when he wrote around 1600: "The witch truly convicted is to be punished with death, the highest degree of punishment, and that by the law of Moses, the *equity* whereof is perpetual."[46] Philip Stubbs (d. 1610), an influential Puritan and author of *An Anatomie of Abuses* asked: "What kind of punishment would you have appointed for these notorious bloody swearers? I would wish (if it pleased God) that it were made death: For we read in the law of God, that whosoever blasphemeth the Lord, was presently stoned to death without all remorce. Which law *judicial* standeth in force to the world's end."[47]

From these sample Puritans—Perkins, Cartwright, and Stubbs—the binding character of the statutes of God's Law lies not in their ancient, Israel-based form (by stoning, after fleeing to cities of refuge, and upon consulting elders in the gates). Nevertheless, in the cases involving capital crimes, the underlying equity continues to require death even in the new covenant era.

As noted earlier, the famed Puritan scholar John Owen thought along these lines:

> Although the institutions and examples of the Old Testament, of the duty of magistrates in the things and about the worship of God, are not, in their whole latitude and extent, to be drawn into rules that should be obligatory to all magistrates now. . . , yet, doubtless, there is something moral in those institutions,

which, being unclothed of their Judaical form, is still binding to all in the like kind, as to some analogy and proportion. Subduct from those administrations what was proper to, and lies upon the account of, the church and nation of the Jews, and what remains upon the general notion of a church and nation must be everlastingly binding.[48]

The modern theonomist would agree that that which is "expired" in the judicial laws are those literal elements structuring it for Israel as a nation: the particular land arrangements which allowed for cities of refuge, blood avengers, elders in the gates, stoning, levirate marriages, and the like. Or those constructions applying to the peculiar ancient circumstances, the accidental historical and cultural factors of Israel: fences around rooftops, goring oxen, flying axheads, and so forth. The Westminster Standards are clearly sympathetic to the theonomic viewpoint.

Confessional Function

My final observation on the historical and Confessional nature of the theonomic argument will focus on the charge of theonomy's alleged novelty in the arrangement of God's Law.

Notice how David C. Jones, a reformed, anti-theonomic, PCA (Presbyterian Church in America) theologian, introduces theonomy into his discussion of Biblical Christian ethics:

> For all its wide acceptance, the tripartite division of the Mosaic law has been seriously challenged in recent years by the theonomy movement in Reformed social ethics. . . . Bahnsen himself favors a bipartite division between the moral law (consisting of general precepts and illustrative applications) and the ceremonial law (consisting of typological and separational precepts).[49]

Perhaps the most vigorous argument against theonomy from this perspective is by another PCA theologian, J. Ligon Duncan. Earlier I cited his summary reasons for dismissing theonomy as a valid confessional system: Theonomists fail "to appreciate the Biblical, theological genius of the Assembly's categorization."[50] Duncan is concerned that theonomy reduces the categories of Law from three (moral, ceremonial, judicial) to two (moral and ceremonial) in order to provide justification for the continuance of the civil law on the coattails, as it were, of the moral law.

In a paper in which he discusses "the theological justification of theo-nomic ethics," Duncan's first point ("Espousal of Twofold Division of the Law") begins:

> Reconstructionists identify the most significant distinction be-tween Old Covenant laws as twofold: moral and ceremonial. Historically speaking, this means a functional denial (most commonly in the form of a reinterpretation) of the traditional Reformed threefold division of the law—moral, civil and cere-monial—(cf. Westminster Confession of Faith 19:3-5) and, alternatively, the espousal of a twofold division—moral and cer-emonial (or restorative).[51]

He complains:

> Theologically, it involves an attempt to identify all non-ceremonial Old Covenant law with the moral law (summarized in the ten commandments) in such a way that they constitute a unity. Hence, if one accepts this identification, and grants that the moral law remains authoritative in the new covenant era, so also must one grant that [sic] the enduring validity all [sic] other non-ceremonial law.[52]

Self-refuting Argument

Before I begin my response, I must mention a surprising aspect of Duncan's argument. He complains of Bahnsen's two-fold division: "Is it as easy to distinguish civil and ceremonial law in the Torah as Bahnsen seems to suggest?"[53] This complaint is altogether disingenuous:

1) Bahnsen and theonomists do *not* suggest the task is easy. Quite the con-trary, we readily admit the difficulty of sorting out the laws appropriately. What is more, who is not aware of the enormous difficulties of sorting out *Paul's own* position on the Law—sometimes affirming it (Rom. 3:31; 7:12); sometimes decrying it (Gal. 3:24-25; 1 Cor. 9:20-21)—despite his writing in the New Testament? The ease of sorting out Law issues in Scripture is not an essential precondition of the Biblical nature of an ethical position.

2) What is worse, *this complaint can apply just as easily against the three-fold division of the* Confession! Everyone can easily discern the Ten Com-mandments, which are clearly enumerated in Scripture and distinguished as the moral law (cf. Deut. 4:13; 10:4). But Duncan himself admits a

difficulty sorting out the ceremonial and judicial laws. *Nevertheless* the Confession does distinguish those categories in WCF 19:3 and 19:4. If the tripartite division of the law is a foundational reformed position, as suggested by Duncan; and if the task of sorting out judicial and ceremonial laws is "difficult," even for Duncan; how are theonomists in any greater difficulty than anti-theonomists?

Now allow me to respond to the overall complaint of the novelty of the bi-partite tendency of theonomy. *First*, Duncan is quite mistaken when he speaks of the categorizing of the law into three divisions as due to the "theological genius" of the Assembly. As a matter of historical record: this three-fold distinction was not first formulated at the Westminster Assembly. Over a century prior to the assembly Calvin noted: "We must bear in mind that common division of the whole law of God published by Moses into moral, ceremonial, and judicial laws" (4:20:14). In Calvin's day the tri-partite division was "common."

False Antithesis

Secondly, Duncan's objection involves him in a false antithesis. He allows only one categorization of the Law, the tri-partite division enunciated in WCF 19, as if this necessarily precluded any other convenient categorization, even by Confessional adherents. But may the law not be categorized in various ways according to various needs, even while holding to the historic three-fold categorization at one level? That is, though we may categorize the law in the common tripartite manner, may we not still make the further observation that judicial laws—laws calling for a state response to public crime—are *moral*? If they are not, then are they immoral? Amoral?

Though the Ten Commandments compose the moral law, yet they themselves can be broken down into religious (God-ward) and social (man-ward) duties without affecting their unity or overall classification as moral. The Confession, as 19:1, teaches that there are "ten commandments . . . written in two tables: the first four commandments containing our duty towards God; and the other six, our duty to man."

Does not the Confession itself break down the ceremonial law into smaller components? In the section dealing with the ceremonial law, the divines find both typical and moral laws within the ceremonial: "God was pleased to give to the people of Israel, as a church under age, ceremonial laws, containing several *typical* ordinances, partly of worship, prefiguring Christ, His graces, actions, sufferings, and benefits; and partly, holding forth divers instructions of *moral* duties" (19:3).

Similarly, may we not legitimately classify the inhabitants of the physical world in terms of living and non-living entities? But may we not in another sense further distribute living entities into classifications as humans, animals, and plants, without contradicting the larger class of "living"? Are not lower and higher levels of categorizations common in biology: phylum, class, order, family, genus, species, and variety?

And what are we to make of Presbyterian theologian Charles Hodge's statement claiming there are *four* "different kinds of laws"?[54] Or of A. A. Hodge's observation made while expounding WCF 19: "All the divine laws belong to one or other of four classes"?[55]

Historical Reality

Third, historically Reformed scholars have recognized an underlying two-fold character in God's three-fold Law. In fact, "Augustine in addressing this issue subjected the law of Moses to a bipartite analysis (moral and symbolical)."[56] In his *Reply to Faustus the Manichaean* he formulates his view: "The moral precepts of the law are observed by Christians; the symbolical precepts were properly observed during the time that things now revealed were prefigured."[57]

Calvin himself noted that there is a certain ambiguity in the tripartite division of the Law, which results from the mixed character of the judicial and ceremonial with the moral. In his *Institutes* (4:20:14) he wrote:

> And we must consider each of these parts, that we may understand what there is in them that pertains to us, and what does not. In the meantime, let no one be concerned over the small point that ceremonial and judicial laws pertain also to morals. For the ancient writers who taught this division, although they were not ignorant that these two latter parts had some bearing upon morals, still, because these could be changed or abrogated while morals remained untouched, did not call them moral laws. They applied this name only to the first part without which the

true holiness of morals cannot stand, nor an unchangeable rule of right living.

Thomas Gilbert (1610-1673), a Puritan in the Westminster era, observed regarding the three-fold nature of God's law:

> There were three laws among the Jews, the ceremonial, judicial, and moral laws. I suppose the judicial law, as to the pains of it, was a fence and guard to the ceremonial and moral law. . . . So far as the judicial law was a fence and outworking to the ceremonial law it is fallen with the ceremonial law. So far as it was a fence and outworking of the moral law it stands with the moral law, and that still binds upon men. So [the part of] the judicial law that was a fence to that, is still the duty of magistrates.[58]

Alexander Shields (1660-1685), another Westminster era Puritan, argued in a manner assuming a more basic two-fold division of the law: "We are obliged to cut off idolaters. The idolaters should be put to death, according to the Law of God; and those penal statutes in the Old Testament are not abrogated yet, for they are moral."[59]

Thus, Bahnsen's classification of the law is not antithetical to the Westminster classification. It operates at a different level of categorization. Neither is his classification anti-historical. Duncan's first charge against Bahnsen is without merit.

Conclusion

Upon careful historical and confessional analysis, it would appear that a strong case can be made for the reformed legitimacy of the theonomic position. In the final analysis, then, perhaps Kline has chosen the wisest ecclesiastical way to respond to theonomy: Revise the Confession. With such a revision, ecclesiastics would be relieved of the necessity of arguing Biblically about theonomy; they could constitutionally define theonomy out of order—dismissing both modern theonomists as well as the original framers of the Westminster Standards themselves.

ENDNOTES

1 The work was actually completed in 1971 as R. J. Rushdoony's Foreword indicates. For a brief history of *Theonomy*, see: Greg L. Bahnsen, *No Other Standard: Theonomy and Its Critics*. Tyler, Tex.: Institute for Christian Economics, 2–5, especially noting footnote 1.

2 Bahnsen, *No Other Standard*, 3.

3 David K. Watson, "The Christian Reconstruction/Theonomy Movement," *Outlook* 38, Nov., 1988, 13.

4 J. Ligon Duncan, "Moses' Law for Modern Government: The Intellectual and Sociological Origins of the Christian Reconstructionist Movement" presented October 15, 1994 to the Social Science History Association, Atlanta, Georgia, 21.

5 Meredith G. Kline, "Comments on an Old-New Error: A Review Article," *Westminster Theological Journal* 41:1, Fall, 1978: 173.

6 R. Laird Harris, "Theonomy in Christian Ethics: A Review of Greg L. Bahnsen's Book," in *Presbuterion: Covenant Seminary Review*, 5:1, Spring, 1979, 1.

7 Sinclair Ferguson, "An Assembly of Theonomists" in Will S. Barker and W. Robert Godfrey, *Theonomy: An Informed Critique*. Grand Rapids: Zondervan, Ferguson, 323–324.

8 Ferguson, 346–47.

9 D. Clair Davis, "A Challenge to Theonomy," in Will S. Barker and W. Robert Godfrey, *Theonomy: An Informed Critique*. Grand Rapids: Zondervan, 1990, 394.

10 Ferguson, 346–47.

11 Ferguson, 348.

12 Ferguson, 327.

13 William Hetherington, *History of the Westminster Assembly of Divines*. Edmonton: Still Waters Revival, rep. 1991 [1856], 400.

14 Hetherington, 401.

15 Cited in Christopher Coldwell, ed., *Anthology of Presbyterian & Reformed Literature*. Dallas: Naphtali, 1991, 182–183.

16 Hetherington, *History of the Westminster Assembly of Divines*, 394.

17 Samuel Rutherford, *Lex, Rex, or The Law and the Prince*. Harrisonburg, VA: Sprinkle, rep. 1982 [1644], 4.

18 Rutherford, 232.

19 Samuel Rutherford, *The Due Right of Presbyteries, or, A Peaceable Plea*. London: 1644, 358. Cited in Foulner, *Theonomy and the Westminster Confession*, 16.

20 See: *Minutes of the Eleventh General Assembly of the Presbyterian Church in America*, 1983, 97, "Advice of the Sub-Committee on Judicial Business."

21 Jeremiah Burroughs, *Irenicum, to the Lovers of Truth and Peace*, London, 1646, 19–20.

22 Herbert Palmer, *The Glasse of God's Providence towards His Faithfull Ones*. Sermon before Parliament, Aug. 13, 1644, 52.

23 William Reyner, *Babylons Ruining: Earthquake and the Restoration of Zion*. A sermon preached before the House of Commons, August 28, 1644.

24 Richard Vines, *The Authours, Nature and Danger of Haeresie. Laid open in a sermon Preached before the Honourable House of Commons*, London, 1647, 64.

25 Martin A. Foulner, *Theonomy and the West-minster Confession.* Edinburgh: Marpet, 1997.

26 George W. Knight, III, "The Scriptures Were Written for Our Instruction," in *Journal of the Evangelical Theological Society*, 39, March, 1996, 3–14.

27 See: Michael Dennis Gabbert, "A Historical Evaluation of the Christian Reconstruction-ism Based on the Inherent Inviability of Se-lected Theocratic Models," PH.D. dissertation: Southwestern Baptist Theological Seminary, 1991. Jack W. Sawyer, Jr., "Moses and the Magistrate: Aspects of Calvin's Political The-ory in Contemporary Focus," Master's Thesis: Westminster Theological Seminary, 1986.

28 Calvin there is denouncing the radical Ana-baptists who would seek to overthrow govern-ments not properly established. See: James B. Jordan, "Calvinism and 'The Judicial Law of Moses'," in Gary North, ed., *Journal of Chris-tian Reconstruction*, 5:3, Winter, 1978–79, 22ff. Sawyer, Jr., "Moses and the Magistrate: Aspects of Calvin's Political Theory" in *Con-temporary Focus*, ch. 4.

29 John Calvin, *Commentaries on the Four Last Books of Moses*, vol. 3. Grand Rapids: Baker, rep. 1979, 78.

30 Philip Schaff, *History of the Christian Church*, vol. 8, 3rd ed. Grand Rapids: Eerdmans, rep. n.d. [1910], 792.

31 Gentry, "Church Sanctions in the Epistle to the Hebrews," in Gary North, ed. *Theonomy: An Informed Response.* Tyler, Tex.: Institute for Christian Economics, 1991, especially the sec-tion "Penal Sanctions and Apostasy," 189–92.

32 Martin Bucer, *De Regno Christi*, trans. and ed. by Wilhelm Pauck, *The Library of Chris-tian Classics*, vol. 19. Philadelphia: Westmin-ster, 1954, 378.

33 Bucer, 383.

34 John Knox, "The First Blast of the Trumpet against the monstrous Regiment of Women,"

in *Selected Writings of John Knox.* Dallas: Presbyterian Heritage, 1995, 408.

35 Heinrich Bullinger, as cited by Martin Foulner, *Theonomy and the Westminster Confession*, 52.

36 Thomas Shepard, *The Morality of the Sab-bath* in *The Works of Thomas Shepard*, vol. 3. Boston: Doctrinal Tract and Book Society, 1853, 53ff.

37 James Durham, *The Law Unsealed; or, a Prac-tical Exposition of the Ten Commandments.* Glasgow: 1798, 22.

38 James Durham, *Lectures on Job.* Dallas: Naph-tali, 1995, 170.

39 The italicized portion both emphasizes the important phrase and highlights the Amer-ican deletion from the Confession.

40 Bracketed sentence omitted in American version.

41 Originally the divines submitted the Stan-dards to the Parliament without Scripture texts. The House of Commons returned them and required that such be added. The reluc-tance of the Assembly was due to the time pressures they were under, rather than to any principial opposition to appending them. See: Robert Baillie, *Letters and Journals*, vol. 2. Edinburgh: Robert Ogle, 1841, 415ff.; and Alexander F. Mitchell, *The Westminster Assembly: Its History and Standards.* Lon-don: James Nisbet, 1883, 367–368.

42 Stephen Pribble, *Scripture Index to the West-minster Standards.* Dallas: Presbyterian Heri-tage, 1994, 9–13.

43 Donald Remillard, *Contemporary Edition of the Westminster Confession of Faith.* Ligonier, Penn.: Presby Press, 1988, v.

44 Thomas Hutchinson, *The History of the Colony and Province of Massachusetts Bay*, ed., Lawrence S. Mayo. New York: Kraus, rep. 1970 [1864], 2:354.

45 From Thomas Cartwright's *Second Reply*, cited in *Works of John Whitgift*. Parker Society ed., Cambridge: University Press, 1851, I:270.

46 Cited in Rossell H. Robbins, *Encyclopedia of Witchcraft and Demonology*. New York: Crown, 1959, 382.

47 Philip Stubbs, *An Anatomie of Abuses* (1583), as cited in Thomas Rogers, *Exposition of the Thirty-nine Articles*. Cambridge: Cambridge University Press, 1854, 90.

48 John Owen, *The Works of John Owen*, vol. 8. London: Banner of Truth, rep. 1967, 394.

49 David Clyde Jones, *Biblical Christian Ethics*. Grand Rapids: Baker, 1994, 112, 113.

50 Duncan, "Moses' Law for Modern Government," 21n.

51 Duncan, 8.

52 Duncan, 8.

53 Duncan, 9.

54 Charles Hodge, *Systematic Theology*. Grand Rapids: Eerdmans, rep. 1973, 3:267.

55 A. A. Hodge, *A Commentary on the Confession of Faith*. Philadelphia: Presbyterian Board of Publication and Sabbath-School Work, 1923, 338.

56 David Clyde Jones, *Biblical Christian Ethics*. Grand Rapids: Baker, 1994, 110.

57 Augustine, "Reply to Faustus the Manichaean," in Philip Schaff, ed., *A Select Library of the Nicene and Post-Nicene Fathers of the Christian Church*, vol. 10. New York: Scribners, 1901, 2.

58 Thomas Gilbert, *Puritanism and Liberty Being the Army Debates* (1647–1649). Cited in Foulner, *Theonomy and the Westminster Confession*, 44.

59 Alexander Shields, *Some Notes or Heads of a Preface and of a Lecture*. Sermon at Distinckom-Hill in the Parish of Gaastoun, Apr. 15, 1688.

CHAPTER EIGHT

Revelation of Jesus Christ

An Overview of
The Book of Revelation

Below I will survey the issues regarding Revelation's date of composition and theme. In that establishing Revelation's time of origin is a crucial issue for the proper interpretation of the book, I will begin with a brief presentation of the case for the early dating of Revelation. In that understanding, the flow and purpose of Revelation should be among the interpreter's leading goals, I will deal a little more at length with the question of the book's theme. Once the question of when Revelation was written is resolved, I believe the question of what it is about comes into better focus.

The Date of Composition

There are two basic positions on the dating of Revelation, although each has several slight variations. The current majority position is the late-date view. This view holds that the Apostle John wrote Revelation toward the close of the reign of Domitian Caesar—about A.D. 95 or 96. The minority viewpoint today is the early-date position. Early-date advocates hold that Revelation was written by John prior to the destruction of Jerusalem and the Temple in A.D. 70.

I hold that Revelation was produced prior to the death of Nero in June, A.D. 68, and even before the formal engagement of the Jewish War by Vespasian in Spring, A.D. 67. My position is that Revelation was written in A.D. 65 or 66. This would be after the outbreak of the Neronic persecution in November, 64, and before the engagement of Vespasian's forces in Spring of 67.

Though the late-date view is the majority position today, this has not always been the case. In fact, it is the opposite of what prevailed among leading Biblical scholars a little over seventy-five years ago. Late-date advocate William Milligan conceded in 1893 that "recent scholarship has, with little exception, decided in favour of the earlier and not the later date." [1] Two-decades later in 1910 early-date advocate Philip Schaff could still confirm Milligan's report: "The early date is now accepted by perhaps the majority of scholars." [2]

In the 1800s and early 1900s the early-date position was held by such worthies as Moses Stuart, Friederich Düsterdieck, B. F. Westcott, F. J. A. Hort, Joseph B. Lightfoot, F. W. Farrar, Alfred Edersheim, Philip Schaff, Milton Terry, Augustus Strong, and others. Though in eclipse presently, the early-date view has not totally faded away, however. More recent advocates of the early-date include Albert A. Bell, F. F. Bruce, Rudolf Bultmann, C. C. Torrey, J. A. T. Robinson, J. A. Fitzmeyer, J. M. Ford, C. F. D. Moule, Cornelis Vanderwaal, Stephen G. Smalley, Roland H. Worth, Iain Boxall, and others.

But rather than committing an *ad verecundiam* fallacy, let us move beyond any appeal to authority and consider very briefly the argument for the early date of Revelation. Due to time constraints, I will succinctly engage only three of the internal indicators of composition date. The internal evidence should hold priority for the evangelical Christian in that it is evidence from Revelation's self-witness. I will only summarily allude to the arguments from tradition before concluding this matter. Generally it is the practice of late-date advocates to begin with the evidence from tradition, while early-date advocates start with the evidence from self-witness.

The Temple in Revelation 11

In Revelation 11:1, 2 (KJV) we read:

> And there was given me a reed like unto a rod: and the angel stood, saying, Rise, and measure the temple of God, and the altar, and

them that worship therein. But the court which is without the temple leave out, and measure it not; for it is given unto the Gentiles: and the holy city shall they tread under foot forty and two months.

Here we find a Temple standing in a city called "the holy city." Surely John, a Christian Jew, has in mind historical Jerusalem when he speaks of "the holy city." This seems necessary in that John is writing scripture and Jerusalem is frequently called the "holy city" in the Bible. For example: Isaiah 48:2; 52:1; Daniel 9:24; Nehemiah 11:1, 18; Matthew 4:5; 27:53. In addition, verse 8 informs us that this is the city where "also our Lord was crucified." This was historical Jerusalem, according to the clear testimony of Scripture (Luke 9:22; 13:33; 17:11; 19:28). Interestingly, historical Jerusalem is never mentioned by name in Revelation. This may be due to the name "Jerusalem" meaning "city of peace." In Revelation, the meanings of specific names are important to the dramatic imagery. And so it would be inappropriate to apply the name "Jerusalem" to the city upon which woe and destruction are about to be wreaked.

Now what Temple stood in Jerusalem? Obviously the Jewish Temple ordained of God, wherein the Jewish sacrifices were offered. In the first century, it was known as Herod's Temple. This reference to the Temple must be that historical structure for four reasons:

1) It was located in Jerusalem, as the text clearly states in verse 8. This can only refer to the Herodian Temple, which appears over and over again in the New Testament record. It was the very Temple which was even the subject of one of Christ's longer prophetic discourses (Matt. 23:37-24:2ff.).

2) Revelation 11:1, 2, written by the beloved disciple and hearer of Christ, seems clearly to draw upon Jesus' statement from the Olivet Discourse. In Luke 21:5-7, the disciples specifically point to the Herodian Temple to inquire of its future; in Revelation 11:1 John specifically speaks of the Temple of God. In Luke 21:6 Jesus tells His disciples that the Temple will soon be destroyed stone by stone. A comparison of Luke 21:24 and Revelation 11:2 strongly suggests that the source of Revelation's statement is Christ's word in Luke 21.

• Luke 21:24b: "Jerusalem will be trampled underfoot by the Gentiles until the times of the Gentiles are fulfilled."

- Revelation 11:2b (KJV): "it is given unto the Gentiles: and the holy city shall they tread under foot for forty and two months."

The two passages speak of the same unique event and even employ virtually identical terms.

3) According to Revelation 11:2 Jerusalem and the Temple were to be under assault for a period of forty-two months. We know from history that the Jewish War with Rome was formally engaged in Spring, A.D. 67, and was won with the collapse of the Temple in August, A.D. 70. This is a period of forty-two months, which fits the precise measurement of John's prophecy. Thus, John's prophecy antedates the outbreak of the Jewish War.

4) After the reference to the destruction of the "temple of God" in the "holy city," John later speaks of a "new Jerusalem" coming down out of heaven, which is called the "holy city" (Rev. 21:2) and which does not need a temple (Rev. 21:22). This new Jerusalem is apparently meant to supplant the old Jerusalem with its temple system. The old order Temple was destroyed in August, A.D. 70.

Thus, while John wrote, the Temple was still standing, awaiting its approaching doom. If John wrote this twenty-five years after the Temple's fall it would be terribly anachronous. The reference to the Temple is hard architectural evidence that gets us back into an era pre-A.D. 70.

The Seven Kings in Revelation 17

In Revelation 17:1-6, a vision of a seven-headed beast is recorded. In this vision, we discover strong evidence that Revelation was written before the death of Nero, which occurred on June 8, A.D. 68.

John wrote to be understood. The first of seven benedictions occurs in his introduction: "Blessed is he that readeth, and they that hear the words of this prophecy, and keep those things which are written therein" (Rev. 1:3, KJV). And just after the vision itself is given in Revelation 17:1-6, an interpretive angel appears for the express purpose of explaining the vision: "And the angel said unto me, Wherefore didst thou marvel? I will tell thee the mystery of the woman, and of the beast that carrieth her, which hath the seven heads and ten horns" (Rev. 17:7, KJV). Then in verses 9 and 10 this angel explains the vision: "Here is the mind which hath wisdom. The seven heads are seven mountains, on which the woman sitteth.

And there are seven kings: five are fallen, and one is, and the other is not yet come; and when he cometh, he must continue a short space."

Most evangelical scholars recognize that the seven mountains represent the famed seven hills of Rome. The recipients of Revelation lived under the rule of Rome, which was universally distinguished by its seven hills. How could the recipients, living in the seven historical churches of Asia Minor and under Roman imperial rule, understand anything else but this geographical feature?

But there is an additional difficulty involved. The seven heads have a two-fold referent. We learn also that the seven heads represent a political situation in which five kings have fallen, the sixth is, and the seventh is yet to come and will remain but a short while. It is surely no accident that Nero was the sixth emperor of Rome, who reigned after the deaths of his five predecessors and before the brief rule of the seventh emperor.

Flavius Josephus, the Jewish contemporary of John, clearly points out that Julius Caesar was the first emperor of Rome and that he was followed in succession by Augustus, Tiberius, Caius, Claudius, and Nero (*Antiquities* 18; 19). We discover this enumeration also in other near contemporaries of John: 4 Ezra 11 and 12; *Sibylline Oracles*, books 5 and 8; Barnabas, Epistle 4; Suetonius, *Lives of the Twelve Caesars*; and Dio Cassius' *Roman History*, 5.

The text of Revelation says of the seven kings "five have fallen." The first five emperors are dead, when John writes. But the verse goes on to say "one is." That is, the sixth one is then reigning even as John wrote. That would be Nero Caesar, who assumed imperial power upon the death of Claudius in October, A.D. 54, and remained emperor until June, A.D. 68.

John continues: "The other is not yet come; and when he comes, he must continue a short space." When the Roman Civil Wars broke out in rebellion against him, Nero committed suicide on June 8, A.D. 68. The seventh king was "not yet come." That would be Galba, who assumed power in June, A.D. 68. But he was only to continue a "short space." His reign lasted but six months, until January 15, A.D. 69.

Thus, we see that while John wrote, Nero was still alive and Galba was looming in the near future. Revelation could not have been written after June, A.D. 68, according to the internal political evidence.

The Jews in Revelation

The final evidence from Revelation's self-witness that I will consider is the relationship of the Jew to Christianity in Revelation. And although there are several aspects of this evidence, we will just briefly introduce it. Two important passages and their implications may be referred to illustratively.

First, when John writes Revelation, Christians are tensely mingled with the Jews. Christianity is presenting herself as the true Israel and Christians the real Jews (cp. Gal. 3:6-9, 29; Phil. 3:3; 1 Pet. 2:9). In Revelation 2:9 we read of Jesus' word to one of His churches of the day: "I know your tribulation and your poverty (but you are rich), and the blasphemy by those who say they are Jews and are not, but are a synagogue of Satan."

Who but a Jew would call himself a Jew? But in the early formative history of Christianity, believers are everywhere in the New Testament presented as "Abraham's seed," "the circumcision," "the Israel of God," the "true Jew," etc. We must remember that even Paul, the apostle to the Gentiles, took Jewish vows and had Timothy circumcised. But after the destruction of the Temple (A.D. 70) there was no tendency to intermingling. In fact, the famed Jewish rabbi, Gamaliel II, put a curse on Christians in the daily benediction, which virtually forbad social intermingling.

In Revelation the Jews are represented as emptily calling themselves "Jews." They are not true Jews in the fundamental, spiritual sense, which was Paul's argument in Romans 2. This would suggest a date prior to the final separation of Judaism and Christianity. Christianity was a protected religion under Rome's *religio licita* legislation, as long as it was considered a sect of Judaism. The legal separation of Christianity from Judaism was in its earliest stages, beginning with the Neronic persecution in late A.D. 64. It was finalized both legally and culturally with the Temple's destruction, as virtually all historical and New Testament scholars agree. Interestingly, in the A.D. 80s, the Christian writer Barnabas makes a radical "us/them" division between Israel and the Church (*Epistle of Barnabas*, 13:1).[3]

Second, at the time John writes, things are in the initial stages of a fundamental change. Revelation 3:9 reads: "Behold, I will cause those of the synagogue of Satan, who say that they are Jews, and are not, but lie—I will make them come and bow down at your feet, and make them know that I have loved you."

John points to the approaching humiliation of the Jews, noting that God will vindicate His Church against them. In effect, He would make the Jews to lie down at the Christian's feet. This can have reference to nothing other than the destruction of Israel and the Temple, which was prophesied by Christ. After that horrible event, Christians began making reference to the Temple's destruction as an apologetic and vindication of Christianity. Ignatius (A.D. 107) is a classic example of this in his *Magnesians* 10. There are scores of such references in such writers as Melito, Tertullian, Clement of Alexandria, Lactantius, and others.

There are other arguments regarding the Jewish character of Revelation, such as its grammar, its reference to the twelve tribes, allusions to the priestly system, temple worship, and so forth. The point seems clear enough: When John writes Revelation, Christianity is not divorced from Israel. After A.D. 70 such would not be the case. This is strong sociocultural evidence for a pre-A.D. 70 composition.

External Evidence

Before concluding, I will briefly consider some of the external evidence brought to the debate over Revelation's dating.[4]

Irenaeus. I believe we can make a case for the reconstruction of Irenaeus' famous statement, which is the major late-date evidence from tradition. Writing in about 180 in book 5 of his *Against Heresies*, Irenaeus is dealing with the identification of Revelation's "666," which he applies to the Antichrist:

> We will not, however, incur the risk of pronouncing positively as to the name of Antichrist; for if it were necessary that his name should be distinctly revealed in this present time, it would have been announced by him who beheld the apocalyptic vision. For that was seen no very long time since, but almost in our day, towards the end of Domitian's reign.

Upon first reading, this appears to place Revelation's composition toward the end of Domitian's reign, in about 95 or 96.

Unfortunately, for late-date advocacy the statement "that was seen" (or "it was seen") grammatically may refer either to one of two antecedents. It may refer either to "the apocalyptic vision" (i.e., Revelation) or to "him who beheld the apocalyptic vision" (i.e., John). Greek is an inflected language, containing the pronominal idea in the verb ending. So the verb may legitimately be translated either "it was seen" or "he was seen." If "he was seen" is correct, then this says nothing about the date of Revelation.

Shepherd of Hermas. With a great number of Biblical scholars, I am convinced that the Shepherd of Hermas shows dependence on Revelation. I also believe the Shepherd was written in the late 80s.

Muratorian Canon (mid to late second century). This famous list of canonical books states that John wrote letters to seven churches before Paul finished his church letters, which were to seven different congregations.

Tertullian of Carthage (d. 225). Tertullian relates a tradition that seems to indicate John was banished at about the same time as Peter and Paul were martyred.

Clement of Alexandria (d. 220). Clement informs us that all revelation ceased under Nero's reign. He makes this claim while elsewhere holding that John's Revelation was inspired of God.

Epiphanius of Salamis (d. 403). Epiphanius dates Revelation under Claudius' reign. This is either a wild, unaccountable, and unique error, or it is a reference to Nero by his other name. Nero's full adoptive name was Nero Claudius Caesar.

Syriac tradition. Various Syriac manuscripts specifically assign John's banishment to the reign of Nero.

Cappadocian witness. Arethas interprets many of the prophecies of Revelation as being fulfilled in the Jewish War and Andreas has to combat such interpretations in his day.

Conclusion

I have surveyed the political evidence regarding the Seven Kings, the architectural evidence of the standing Temple, and the socio-cultural evidence of the uneasy Jew/Christian mixture. These suggest Revelation was written prior to the destruction of the Temple in August, 70, and even before the death of Nero Caesar, which occurred on June 8, A.D. 68 I believe we can even press it back before the formal engagement of the Jewish War in February, 67, though not before the outbreak of the Neronic persecution beginning in November, 64.

I believe the early-date of Revelation may be firmly established in the seventh decade of the first century, not the last. Having come to this conclusion, let me now turn to consider:

The Theme of Revelation

When interpreting any book of the Bible, it is important for us to take into account the audience to which it was originally directed. There are at least three factors in Revelation that emphasize the original audience and their historic circumstances. These begin to move us toward a proper conclusion regarding the main point of Revelation. When these are combined with the matter of the expectation of Revelation (with which I will deal below), the proper interpretation becomes evident on the basis of sound hermeneutical principle.

Audience Relevance

First, in Revelation we have clear evidence that John is writing to particular, historic, individual churches that existed in his day. Revelation 1:4a (KJV) reads: "John to the seven churches which are in Asia." In verse 11 he specifically names the seven churches to whom he speaks. We know these are historical cities containing historical churches. These churches are specifically dealt with in terms of their historically and culturally unique circumstances in chapters 2 and 3. Real first-century Christians are being addressed.

Second, as I indicated previously, John writes to these churches in order to be understood. Revelation 1:3 (KJV) reads: "Blessed is he that readeth, and they that hear the words of this prophecy, and keep those things which are written therein." Real first-century Christians are expected to understand and to heed John's message as something most relevant to themselves.

Third, in Revelation, John notes that he and the seven churches have already entered "tribulation" (Rev. 1:9a, KJV): "I John, who also am your brother, and companion in tribulation, and in the kingdom and patience of Jesus Christ, was in the isle that is called Patmos, for the word of God, and for the testimony of Jesus Christ." In Revelation 2 and 3 there are allusions to greater problems brewing on the world scene. Real first-century Christians were to have a deep and personal concern with the era in which they lived.

Contemporary Expectation

It is terribly important that the interpreter of Revelation begin at the first verses of the book and let them lead him to the proper interpretive approach. The truth of the matter is: John specifically states that the prophecies of Revelation, which were written to seven historical churches, would begin coming to pass within a very short period of time. He emphasized this truth in a variety of ways. Let us briefly note his contemporary expectation from two angles.

First, we should note that he varies his manner of expression, as if to avoid any potential confusion as to his meaning. The first of these terms we come upon in Revelation is the Greek word *tachos*, translated "shortly." John is explaining the purpose of his writing in Revelation 1:1a, which reads: "The Revelation of Jesus Christ, which God gave Him to show to His bond-servants, the things which must shortly [*tachos*] take place." This term also occurs in Revelation 2:16; 3:11; and 22:6,7, 12, 20.

Another term John uses is *eggus*, which means "near." In Revelation 1:3 we read: "Blessed is he who reads and those who hear the words of the prophecy, and heed the things which are written in it; for the time is near [*eggus*]." Revelation 22:10 (KJV) reads: "And He saith unto me, 'Seal not the sayings of the prophecy of this book: for the time is at hand [*eggus*].'" The import of *eggus* in our context is clearly that of temporal nearness.

Second, John emphasizes his anticipation of the soon occurrence of His prophecy by strategic placement of these time references. He places his boldest time statements in both the introduction and conclusion to Revelation. The statement of expectancy is found twice in the first three verses: Revelation 1:1 & 3. The same idea is found four times in his concluding remarks: Revelation 22:6, 7, 12, 20. It is as if John carefully bracketed the entire work to avoid any confusion. It is important to note that these statements occur in the more historical and didactic sections of Revelation, before and after the major dramatic-symbolic visions.

With the particular audience emphasized along with the message of imminent expectation, I do not see how a first-century fulfillment of Revelation can be doubted. This view of a first-century fulfillment for the bulk of Revelation is called "preterism," from the Latin *praeteritus* which means "past."

Theme Statement

The theme of Revelation is found in Revelation 1:7: "Behold, He is coming with the clouds, and every eye will see Him, even those who pierced Him; and all the tribes of the earth will mourn over Him. Even so. Amen."

I am convinced that the apocalyptic language in this passage must be applied to Christ's judgment coming upon Israel, rather than to the Second Advent at the end of temporal history. The events of A.D. 70, like those associated with the collapse of Babylon, Egypt, and other nations, are typological foreshadowings of the consummational Second Advent.

Cloud-comings are frequent prophetic emblems in the Old Testament. They serve as indicators of divine visitations of judgment upon ancient, historical nations. God "comes" in judicial judgment upon Israel's enemies in general (Ps. 18:7-15; 104:3), upon Egypt (Isa. 19:1), upon disobedient Israel in the Old Testament (Joel 2:1, 2), and so forth. To cite one example, Isaiah 19:1 (KJV) says: "Behold, the LORD rideth upon a swift cloud, and shall come into Egypt: and the idols of Egypt shall be moved at His presence, and the heart of Egypt shall melt in the midst of it."

A coming of Christ in judgment upon Israel is clearly taught in parabolic form by Christ in Matthew 21:40, 41, 43, 45 (NKJV™):

> "Therefore, when the owner of the vineyard comes, what will he do to those vinedressers?" They said to Him, "He will destroy those wicked men miserably, and lease his vineyard to other vinedressers, who will render to him the fruits in their seasons." ..."Therefore I say to you, The kingdom of God will be taken

from you and given to a nation bearing the fruits of it." ... Now when the chief priests and Pharisees heard His parables, they perceived that He was speaking of them.

This surely speaks of the destruction of the Jerusalem of the chief priests and Pharisees of Jesus' day. And it will occur "when the Lord of the vineyard comes." This is the judgment-coming of Christ in A.D. 70.

For several reasons I am convinced that Revelation 1:7 also refers to His coming in judgment upon Israel.

First, this coming is a judgment-coming upon "those who pierced Him." The New Testament emphatically points to first century Israel as responsible for crucifying Christ. Israel forced the hand of the Roman procurator, Pontius Pilate, when the Jews cried out in John 19:15: "'Away with Him, away with Him, crucify Him.' Pilate saith unto them, 'Shall I crucify your King?' The chief priests answered, 'We have no king but Caesar.'" See also: Acts 2:22-23, 36; 3:13-15; 5:30; 7:52; 1 Thess. 2:14-15.

Second, Revelation 1:7 states that as a consequence of this judgment "all the tribes [*phule*] of the Land [*he ge*] will mourn." "The Land" is a familiar designation for Israel's Promised Land. And as is well known, Israel was divided into twelve tribes. In fact, Revelation 7 has the marking out of 144,000 from among the specifically designated twelve tribes of Israel before the winds of destruction blow upon the "land." When Revelation broadens the definition of "tribes" to incorporate non-Jews, it does not speak of "the land" (*he ge*), but "the nations" (*ethnoi*).

Third, Jesus even told the first-century Jewish leaders that they would witness this judgment-coming. In Matthew 26:63-64 (KJV), we read: "But Jesus held His peace. And the high priest answered and said unto Him, 'I adjure thee by the living God, that thou tell us whether thou be the Christ, the Son of God.' Jesus saith unto him, 'Thou hast said: nevertheless I say unto you, Hereafter shall ye see the Son of man sitting on the right hand of power, and coming in the clouds of heaven.'"

This coming, dealt with at length in Matthew 24:1-34 (KJV) was to occur in His generation. Matthew 24:30 and 34 read: "And then shall appear the sign of the Son of man in heaven: and then shall all the tribes of the earth mourn, and they shall see the Son of man coming in the clouds of heaven with power and great glory.... Verily I say unto you, This generation shall not pass, till all these things be fulfilled."

Drawing this information together, we can compare it with the historical facts of the era as follows:

The Jewish War with Rome from 67 to 70 brought about the deaths of tens of thousands of the Jews in Judea, and the enslavement of thousands upon thousands more. The Jewish historian Flavius Josephus, who was an eye-witness, records that 1.1 million Jews perished in the siege of Jerusalem.

But as awful as the Jewish loss of life was, the utter devastation of Jerusalem, the final destruction of the temple, and the conclusive cessation of the sacrificial system were lamented even more. The covenantal significance of the loss of the temple stands as the most dramatic outcome of the War. It was an unrepeatable loss, for the temple has never been rebuilt. The old covenant era was forever closed. Hence, any Jewish calamity after A.D. 70 would pale in comparison to the redemptive-historical significance of the loss of the temple. Thus, the theme stated in Revelation 1:7 fits perfectly the events which actually unfolded in that era.

Thematic Character

Before we can actually develop the flow of Revelation, we need to ascertain the identity of a major character in the drama presented: Who is the harlot identified in Revelation 17?

> So he carried me away in the Spirit into the wilderness. And I saw a woman sitting on a scarlet beast which was full of names of blasphemy, having seven heads and ten horns.... And on her forehead a name was written: MYSTERY, BABYLON THE GREAT, THE MOTHER OF HARLOTS AND OF THE ABOMINATIONS OF THE EARTH. (Rev. 17:3, 5, NKJV™)

Some have thought that the harlot is representative of the city of Rome[5] because she is here seen resting upon the seven hills and she is called "Babylon." But since the Beast itself represents Rome, it would seem redundant to have the woman representing the same. Neither does the name "Babylon" historically belong to either Rome or Jerusalem, and thus cannot be proof that the city is Rome rather than

Jerusalem. I am convinced beyond any doubt that this harlot is Jerusalem.

First, in Revelation 14:8 "Babylon" is called "the great city." The first mention of "the great city" in Revelation 11:8, indisputably points to Jerusalem. There we read that it is the place "where also our Lord was crucified" (cp. Luke 9:31; 13:33-34; 18:31; 24:18-20).

Her greatness is in regard to her covenantal status in the Old Testament. "Jerusalem" appears in Scripture 623 times. She is called "the city of the great king" (Ps. 48:2; Matt. 5:35), "the city of God" (Ps. 46:4; 48:1; 87:3), "the joy of the whole earth" (Ps. 48:2; Lam. 2:15), and other such laudable names. She is even called "the great city" elsewhere in Scripture: "People from many nations will pass by this city and will ask one another, 'Why has the LORD done such a thing to this great city?'" (Jer. 22:8, NIV). "How deserted lies the city, once so full of people! How like a widow is she, who once was great among the nations! She who was queen among the provinces has now become a slave" (Lam. 1:1, NIV).

Even pagan writers speak highly of Jerusalem. Tacitus calls it "a famous city" (*Histories,* 5:2). Pliny the Elder writes that Jerusalem was "by far the most famous city of the ancient Orient" (*Natural History,* 5:14:70). Appian, a Roman lawyer and writer (ca. A.D. 160), calls her "the great city Jerusalem" (*The Syrian Wars,* 50).

Second, the Babylonian harlot is filled with the blood of the saints, according to Revelation 16:6; 17:6; 18:21, 24. For instance, Revelation 18:24 reads: "And in her was found the blood of prophets and of saints and of all who have been slain on the earth." Of course, with the outbreak of the Neronic persecution in AD 64, which had just gotten under way, Rome was stained with the blood of the saints. Yet Rome had only recently entered the persecuting ranks of God's enemies. Throughout Acts, Jerusalem is portrayed as the persecutor and Rome as the protector of Christianity.[6] Furthermore, Rome was not guilty of killing any of the Old Testament prophets, as was Jerusalem.[7] Before his stoning, Stephen rebukes Jerusalem: "Which of the prophets have not your fathers persecuted? And they have slain them who showed before of the coming of the Just One, of whom ye have been now the betrayers and murderers" (Acts 7:52, KJV).

In the context of the Olivet Discourse, Jesus reproaches Jerusalem. Matthew 23:34-35 (NKJV™) reads: "Therefore, indeed, I send you prophets, wise men, and scribes: some of them you will kill and crucify, and some of them you will scourge in your synagogues and persecute from city to city, that on you may come all the righteous blood shed on the earth, from the blood of righteous Abel to the blood of Zechariah, son of Berechiah, whom you murdered between the temple and the altar."

Throughout Revelation it is the slain Lamb who acts in judgment upon His slayers, the Jews. "Then I saw a Lamb, looking as if it had been slain, standing in the center of the throne, encircled by the four living creatures and the elders. He had seven horns and seven eyes, which are the seven spirits of God sent out into all the earth" (Rev. 5:6, NIV; cp. 5:12; 13:8). This Lamb is mentioned twenty-seven times in Revelation.[8] And Jerusalem literally called down judgment upon herself for slaying the Lamb of God: "All the people answered, 'Let His blood be on us and on our children!'" (Matt. 27:25, NIV).

Third, the harlot is arrayed in the Jewish priestly colors of scarlet, purple, and gold described in Exodus 28.[9] These colors were also found in the Temple: Josephus carefully describes Jerusalem's Temple tapestry as "Babylonian tapestry in which blue, purple, scarlet and linen were mingled" (*Wars*, 5:5:4). He does so while giving the color decor of the Temple much emphasis and elaboration.

The harlot even has a blasphemous inscription on her forehead that gives a negative portrayal of the holy inscription which the Jewish high priest wore. On the high priest's forehead we read: "Holy to the LORD" (Exod. 28:36-38). On the harlot's forehead we read: "Mystery, Babylon the Great, the Mother of Harlots and of the Abominations of the Earth" (Rev. 17:5, KJV). And she has a gold cup in her hand, as did the high priest on the Day of Atonement, according to the Jewish Talmud.[10] Interestingly, the Temple's main door had on it golden vines with great clusters of grapes (from which wine is derived). The golden grape clusters on the vine were very prominent, being the size of a man (Josephus, *Wars*, 5:5:4). These are suggestive of the golden cup to be filled with blood.

Fourth, there is an obvious literary contrast between the harlot and the chaste bride. This juxtaposition suggests an intentional contrast between the Jerusalem below (Rev. 11:8) and the Jerusalem above (Rev. 21:2). This is not unfamiliar to writers of Scripture (cp. Gal. 4:24ff.; Heb. 12:18ff.).

When you compare Revelation 17:2-5 and Revelation 21:1ff., the contrast provides a remarkable negative and positive image. And we must remember that the bride is specifically called the "New Jerusalem" from heaven (Rev. 21:1-2). Consider:

John is introduced to the harlot and to the bride in a similar fashion:

Revelation 17:1 (KJV): "And there came one of the seven angels which had the seven vials, and talked with me, saying unto me, 'Come hither; I will shew unto thee the judgment of the great whore that sitteth upon many waters.'"

Revelation 21:9 (KJV): "And there came unto me one of the seven angels which had the seven vials full of the seven last plagues, and talked with me, saying, 'Come hither, I will shew thee the bride, the Lamb's wife.'"

The two women are contrasted as to character.

Revelation 17:1 (KJV): "Come here, I will shew unto thee the judgment of the great whore that sitteth upon many waters."

Revelation 21:9 (KJV): "Come hither, I will shew thee the bride, the Lamb's wife."

The two women are seen in contrasting environments to which John is carried by the angel.

Revelation 17:3 (KJV): "So he carried me away in the spirit into the wilderness and I saw a woman sit upon a scarlet coloured beast."

Revelation 21:10 (KJV): "And he carried me away in the spirit to a great and high mountain, and shewed me that great city, the holy Jerusalem, descending out of heaven from God."

The dress of each is detailed and contrasted:

Revelation 17:4 (KJV): "And the woman was arrayed in purple and scarlet colour, and decked with gold and precious stones and pearls, having a golden cup in her hand full of abominations and filthiness of her fornication."

Revelation 19:8; 21:11: "And to her was granted that she should be arrayed in fine linen, clean and white: for the fine linen is the righteousness of saints. . . . Having the glory of God: and her light was like unto a stone most precious, even like a jasper stone, clear as crystal."

Fifth, Jerusalem had previously been called by pagan names quite compatible with the designation "Babylon." In Revelation 11:8 (NIV) she was called "spiritually Sodom and Egypt." Isaiah did the same to her in

Isaiah 1 where he called Jerusalem "Sodom and Gomorrah." The idea is that rather than conducting herself as the wife of God, she had become one of His enemies like Sodom, Egypt, and Babylon.

The fact that the harlot is seated on the seven-headed Beast (obviously representative of Rome) indicates not identity with Rome, but alliance with Rome against Christianity. The Jews demanded Christ's crucifixion and constantly agitated against the Christians to get the Romans involved in their persecution (cp. Matt. 23:37ff.; John 19:15-16; Acts 17:7).

Thematic Flow

Now we are ready briefly to sketch the thematic idea of Revelation. Not only is Israel's destruction the focus of Revelation, but her judgment is set forth in an interesting and significant covenantal fashion.

Israel as the Wife of God

We must remember that in the Old Testament Israel was graciously taken by God to be His covenantal wife. Oftentimes the prophets mention the covenantal marriage relation between God and Israel.

- Jeremiah 3:14 (KJV): "Turn, O backsliding children, saith the LORD; for I am married unto you."

- Ezekiel 16 portrays in beautiful poetic imagery, the husbandly love of God for Israel.

- Ezekiel 16:8 (KJV): "Now when I passed by thee, and looked upon thee, behold, thy time was the time of love; and I spread my skirt over thee, and covered thy nakedness: yea, I sware unto thee, and entered into a covenant with thee, saith the LORD GOD, and thou becamest mine."

Other passages alluding to the marriage covenant between God and Israel include: Isaiah 50:1; 54:5; 62:4; Jeremiah 3:20; 31:32; and Ezekiel 16:31-32.

As a covenantal action, Israel's marriage was formally established with proper witnesses. Deuteronomy 31:28 (KJV) reads: "Gather unto me all the elders of your tribes, and your officers, that I may speak these words in their ears, and call heaven and earth to record against them." See also: Deuteronomy 4:26; 30:19.

But as an unfaithful wife, Israel chased after foreign gods, committing spiritual adultery against the Lord. This adulterous infidelity is portrayed in many Old Testament passages.[11] The old covenant prophets served as God's lawyers. As VanGemeren expresses it: "The prophets had spoken as God's covenant prosecutors, bringing God's charge and stating God's verdict."[12] On the basis of God's Law and before witnesses, they legally called upon her to return to her covenantal husband, the Lord God. They often brought a "case" (Heb.: *ribh*) against Israel, calling heaven and earth as witnesses in this heavenly courtroom drama and as per the public confirmation of the covenant.

- Isaiah 1:2 (KJV): "Hear, O heavens, and give ear, O earth: for the LORD hath spoken, I have nourished and brought up children, and they have rebelled against me." Isaiah laments: "How is the faithful city become an harlot!" (Isa. 1:21a).

- Hosea 4:1 (KJV): "Hear the word of the LORD, ye children of Israel: for the LORD hath a controversy with the inhabitants of the land, because there is no truth, nor mercy, nor knowledge of God in the land."

- Micah 6:2 (KJV): "Hear ye, O mountains, the LORD's *controversy*, and ye strong foundations of the earth: for the LORD hath a controversy with His people, and He will plead with Israel." See also Hos. 12:2.

Ultimately, their work was futile in that Israel finally demanded the crucifixion of the Son of God, crying out: "We have no king but Caesar!"

The Divorce Decree against Israel

The dramatic visions of Revelation are framed in such a way as to represent God's judicial divorce decree against Israel. Following upon that, we witness her capital punishment for all sorts of sins, which flowed from her spiritual adultery.

In Revelation 4, God is seen seated on His judicial throne. Interestingly, God's throne is mentioned in eighteen of Revelation's twenty-two chapters. In fact, of the sixty-two appearances of the word "throne" in the New Testament, forty-seven of these are found in Revelation. The judicial element is strong in this book, including references to judgments, witnesses, and the like.

In Revelation 5, a seven-sealed scroll is seen in God's hand, while He is seated upon His throne of justice. The seven-sealed scroll seems to represent God's "bill of divorcement" handed down by the Judge on the throne against Israel. It is known that divorce decrees were written out among the Jews in the Biblical era: Deuteronomy 24:1, 3; Isaiah 50:1; Jeremiah 3:8; Matthew 5:31; 19:7; and Mark 10:4. It is equally certain that marriage was understood in terms of a covenant contract: Proverbs 2:17; Ezekiel 16:8; and Malachi 2:14. That the scroll in Revelation 5-8 would be a bill of divorcement is suggested on the following considerations.

First, in Revelation we have prominent emphases on two particular women, two women who obviously correspond as opposites to one another. The two women are the wicked harlot on the Beast (Rev. 17-18) and the pure bride of Christ (Rev. 21). As I have shown, they correspond with the earthly Jerusalem that was the scene of Christ's crucifixion (Rev. 11:8) and the heavenly Jerusalem which is holy (Rev. 21:10). The flow and drift of the book is the revelation and execution of the legal judgment (Rev. 15:3; 16:5-7) on the fornicating harlot.

Following this, we witness the coming of a virginal bride (Rev. 21), obviously to take her place after a marriage supper (Rev. 19). This fits well with the Pauline imagery in Galatians 4:24ff., where he speaks of the casting out of the one wife (Hagar who is representative of the Jerusalem below) and the taking of the other wife (Sarah who is representative of the Jerusalem above).

Second, the apparent Old Testament background for this imagery is found in Ezekiel and Leviticus. In Ezekiel 2:9-10, Israel's judgment is portrayed as written on a scroll on the front and back and given to Ezekiel. This corresponds perfectly with the scroll in Revelation 5:1. In Ezekiel 2ff., the devastation of Israel is outlined, which corresponds with Revelation 6ff. In Ezekiel 16, Israel is viewed as God's covenant wife which became a harlot that trusted in her beauty and committed fornication (Ezek. 16:15). This is the case with Jerusalem-Babylon in Revelation (Rev. 18:7). She is cast out and judged for this evil conduct.

The reason for seven seals is found in covenantal imagery, as well. The seven seals on Revelation's scroll reflect the seven-fold covenantal judgment God forewarned Israel about in Leviticus 26:18, 21, 24, 28. These judgments are threatened against Israel, if she should forsake God. The seven-fold judgments in Leviticus have a strong influence on the judgment language of Revelation. When these seals are opened, the preliminary judgments begin.

Third, following the "divorce" and judgments associated with it, John turns to see the coming of a new "bride" out of heaven (Rev. 21-22). It would seem that the new bride could not be taken until the harlotrous wife should first be taken care of legally. John himself employs the imagery of the harlot, bride, and marriage feast; this is not being read into the text from outside. Thus, the imagery of divorce well fits the dramatic flow of the work.

The Execution of the Judgments

The punishment in God's Law for adultery is death (Lev. 20:10), which in Biblical law was by stoning. So we discover huge hailstones raining down on Jerusalem in Revelation 16:21 (KJV): "And there fell upon men a great hail out of heaven, every stone about the weight of a talent: and men blasphemed God because of the plague of the hail; for the plague thereof was exceeding great." This was accomplished historically by the tenth legion of the Roman armies:

> The engines [i.e., catapults], that all the legions had ready prepared for them, were admirably contrived; but still more extraordinary ones belonged to the tenth legion: those that threw darts and those that threw stones, were more forcible and larger than the rest, by which they not only repelled the excursions of the Jews, but drove those away that were upon the walls also. Now, the stones that were cast, were of the weight of a talent, and were carried two furlongs and further. The blow they gave was no way to be sustained, not only by those that stood first in the way, but by those that were beyond them for a great space. As for the Jews, they at first watched the coming of the stone, for it was a white colour. (*Wars*, 5:6:3)

Now Israel is not only Jehovah's wife in the Old Testament, but she is to serve Him as a kingdom of priests ministering to the nations (Exod. 19:6). Thus, she is represented in Revelation as being a harlot in priestly garments. Being such, another Old Testament Law comes to bear. Leviticus 21:9 warns, "The daughter of any priest, if she profane herself by playing the harlot, she profaneth her father, she shall be burned with fire." Consequently, we see reference to Israel's being burned with fire in Revelation 17:16: "And the ten horns which thou sawest upon the beast, these shall hate the whore, and shall make her desolate and naked, and shall eat her flesh, and burn her with fire."

Then, having legally disposed of Israel as an harlotrous, priestly wife, Revelation turns to consider a new bride. In Revelation 21, we see a city coming down out of heaven adorned as a spotless virgin bride for her husband. This new city is a *New* Jerusalem. This "New Jerusalem" is the Church, according to Galatians 4:21ff., and Hebrews 12:18ff.

Thus, the theme of Revelation is the execution of God's divorce decree against Israel, her subsequent capital punishment and cremation, followed by His turning to take a new bride, the Church.

Conclusion

In conclusion, I believe that Revelation was written about A.D. 65. I further believe that it speaks to the original Christian audience regarding difficulties they were facing and in explanation of the coming final removal of Jerusalem by God's wrath.

The book is to be understood preteristically, rather than futuristically. We learn this not only from the imminent expectation in the book, but also from its theme (which involves the judgment of the Jews) and due to its leading characters: Jerusalem (as a harlot) and Rome (as a Beast).

ENDNOTES

1 William Milligan, *Discussions on the Apocalypse.* London: Macmillan, 1893, 75.

2 Philip Schaff, *History of the Christian Church*, 3rd ed. Grand Rapids: Eerdmans, 1950 [1910], 1:834.

3 *The Epistle of Barnabas* is a Greek treatise with some features of an epistle containing twenty-one chapters, preserved complete in the fourth century *Codex Sinaiticus* where it appears at the end of the New Testament. It is traditionally ascribed to the Barnabas who is mentioned in the Acts of the Apostles, though some ascribe it to another apostolic father of the same name, a "Barnabas of Alexandria," or simply attribute it to an unknown early Christian teacher. A form of the Epistle 850 lines long is noted in the Latin list of canonical works in the sixth century *Codex Claromontanus.*

4 For further evidence in this regard, please see my: *Before Jerusalem Fell: Dating the Book of Revelation*, 3rd ed. Atlanta: American Vision, 1999.

5 Note that the seven heads of the beast represent seven mountains, which picture the famous seven hills of Rome (Rev. 17:9). The beast is portrayed as having "power" and "great authority" (Rev. 13:2) and as persecuting the saints (Rev. 13:7). For more information see: Kenneth L. Gentry, Jr., *The Beast of Revelation*. Powder Springs, GA: American Vision, 2002.

6 See for example: Acts 4:3; 5:18–33; 6:12; 7:54–60; 8:1ff.; 9:1–4, 13, 23; 11:19; 12:1–3; 13:45–50; 14:2–5, 19; 16:23; 17:5–13; 18:12; 20:3, 19; 21:11, 27; 22:30; 23:12, 20, 27, 30; 24:5–9; 25:2–15; 25:24; 26:21. See also: 2 Cor. 11:24; 1 Thessalonians 2:14–15; Hebrews 10:32–34; Revelation 2:9; 3:9; etc.

7 Jeremiah 2:30; Matthew 5:12; 23:34, 35; Acts 7:52; 1 Thessalonians 2:15.

8 See: Revelation 5:6, 8, 12–13; 6:1, 16; 7:9–10, 14, 17; 12:11; 13:8; 14:1, 4, 10; 15:3; 17:14; 19:7, 9; 21:14, 22–23; 22:1, 3.

9 Cp. Revelation 17:4–5 with Exodus 25:2, 4; 26:1, 31, 36; 27:16; 28:1–2, 5–12, 15, 17–23, 33.

10 Golden bowls were used elsewhere in the Levitical services. See: Exodus 25:29; 37:16, 17.

11 See: Isaiah 1:21; 50:1; 57:8; Jer. 2:2, 20; 3:1–20; 4:30; 11:15; 13:27; Ezekiel 6:9; 16:32; Hosea 1:2; 2:5, 7; 3:3; 4:15; Malachi 2:7.

12 Willem VanGemeren, *The Progress of Redemption: The Story of Salvation from Creation to the New Jerusalem* (Grand Rapids: Zondervan, 1988), 290.

Indexes

$\mathfrak{Subject}$

$\mathfrak{Index}$

Scripture

Index

FIRST FOUR BOOKS PRESENTED BY NORDSKOG PUBLISHING
New series of meaty, tasty, and easily digestible theological offerings!

In 1961, A. W. Tozer opined in *The Knowledge of the Holy* that the way some Christians think about God is sinful. Dr. Arnold Frank in *The Fear of God: A Forgotten Doctrine* confirms that the 21st century church, in the pew as well as the pulpit, continues to regard God as impotent and irrelevant . . . in other words, without godly fear. Dr. Frank, with a theologian's skill and a pastor's heart, walks us through the Scriptures, letting the Word of God speak about the fear of God.

In addition to clear, Biblical exposition, Dr. Frank also weaves in the wise and timeless counsel of the Puritans to help us see how the fear of God is a most needed and practical doctrine.

This book is a skillful and gracious reminder of how we should regard the holy, sovereign Creator.
—Mark Kakkuri, *Editor*

A Whole New World: The Gospel According to Revelation

Greg Uttinger's book is refreshing for its brevity; it does not confuse the reader in the minutia of exposition. It demystifies Revelation by focusing the reader on the big picture. I encourage anyone to read it. The blessing on those who read, hear, and keep the message of Revelation (1:3) was referring to its core message . . . that we serve the risen, victorious Lord of time and eternity. Uttinger's book is faithful to that "Revelation of Jesus Christ" (1:1).
—Mark R. Rushdoony, *President, Chalcedon Foundation*

The author clearly and simply puts forth a very realistic interpretation, taken from Scripture as a whole. He deciphers . . . symbolism from the Word of God and concisely . . . explains the glorious future all believers cherish . . . in anticipation of . . . God's ordained "Whole New World."
—Gerald Christian Nordskog, *Publisher*

God's Ten Commandments: Yesterday, Today, Forever

God gave man Ten Commandments. Every one of them is vital, in all ages. . . . God Himself is the Root of the Moral Law, and perfectly reflects it. . . . It is the very basis of the United States . . . and every other Common Law nation in the world.
—Dr. Francis Nigel Lee, *Author, 2007*

Dr. Lee is a man deeply devoted to God . . . I am happy to commend to your reading Dr. Lee's work. . . .
—The Honorable Roy S. Moore, *former Chief Justice, Alabama Supreme Court, and President of the Foundation for Moral Law, Inc.*

The Battle of Lexington: A Sermon & Eye-witness Narrative
—by Lexington Pastor, Jonas Clark, 1776

With powerful voice Jonas Clark tells of . . . the principles of personal, civil, and religious liberty, and the right of resistance. Today our country perishes for lack of preachers who give their congregations courage to stand and make a difference.—*Introduction* by Rev. Christopher Hoops

Includes biographical information on Pastor Clark, facsimile title page from the original 1776 publication, four classic poems commemorating Paul Revere and the "shot heard 'round the world," and illustration.

 Nordskog Publishing inc.

2716 Sailor Ave., Ventura, CA 93001
Jerry@NordskogPublishing.com
805-642-2070 • 805-276-5129

Printed in the United States
214956BV00002B/1/P

9 780979 673641